THE
MORTGAGE
FREEDOM
PLAYBOOK

THE MORTGAGE FREEDOM PLAYBOOK

Easy & Proven
Step-by-Step Methods

LICI DENG

For information about this title or to order other books and/or electronic media, contact the publisher:

www.themortgagefreedomplaybook.com

ISBNs:
978-1-7361616-0-9 (print)
978-1-7361616-1-6 (eBook)

Printed in the United States of America

Cover design: Susan Olinsky
Editing and interior design: 1106 Design

The publication is designed to provide information that the author believes to be accurate on the subject matter it covers. It is sold with the understanding that the author and publisher are not engaged in rendering legal, financial, or other professional services. The author and publisher will not be responsible for any liability, loss, or risk incurred from the use or application of the contents in this book. A competent professional's services should be sought if one needs expert assistance.

While the author has made every effort to provide accurate internet address at the time of publication, neither the publisher nor the author assumes any responsibility for errors or for changes that occur after publication.

ACKNOWLEDGMENT

To my energetic boys, Zephlan and Kaz: You are the motivation for me to write this book. Many thanks to "Uncle" Steven Rizzo for always being there, ready and willing to help. Finally, a special thanks to a special friend, Monica St. Julien, for being non-judgmental and offering endless support during this journey.

TABLE OF CONTENTS

INTRODUCTION

Would you like to pay off your mortgage in just a few years? In late 2018, I saw a clip of a YouTube video that flashed in front of me about how homeowners can use a Home Equity Line of Credit (HELOC) to pay off their mortgage in 5–7 years. Excited and hopeful, I researched, read blogs, posts, and books, and watched numerous podcasts and YouTube videos hoping to find out how to do it. To my disappointment, I found that the YouTubers and promoters had succeeded in regurgitating the HELOC concept and luring the readers in, but they had failed to show the "HOW" part. There was also no shortage of companies advertising this concept, but it always turned out to be a fee-based program that cost from $500 to upwards of $5,000.

My outstanding mortgage balance at the time was nearly $160,000. According to my lender's schedule, my loan will be matured in 2042. That's 23–24 years away! I couldn't bear the thought of being chained to a long-term debt like that. I was determined to be mortgage-free sooner and set out to "figure it out" myself.

For the remainder of 2018 and early 2019, I spent countless hours, sometimes staying up to 3 a.m., reading about HELOC and learning everything there is to know about its interest calculation and how it differs from conventional mortgage interest. I created Excel models, tested it, adjusted it, and changed it—to 20+ versions. I started to use the model and tracking my payoff while calculating the HELOC interest. While doing so, I continued to correct and improve it until all of the dollars and cents matched to the anticipated mortgage and HELOC statements. At that point, I knew the model worked and that I could use it with confidence.

At times, it was frustrating to work on the HELOC model because after a long day at my 8–5 p.m. job, I had very little energy left to do anything else. It was a balancing act between that and taking care of a family with two young kids.

After 16 months on this journey, I sent in my final payment to the lender on February 14, 2020. It took another six weeks to pay off the HELOC balance. On April 1, 2020, I was mortgage-free and it was no April Fool! Total interest paid to the lender was outrageous prior to these 16 months. I wish I'd had someone to show me how to leverage HELOC to pay off my mortgage sooner and save thousands of dollars in interest payment, like I am going to show you.

You, too, can pay off your 15- or 30-year mortgage in just a few years by following the method described in the chapters ahead. Those of you who are just starting out with your mortgage or are in the first few years of your mortgage payment will gain the most benefits. The best part is that you do not even need to adjust your lifestyle or need an extra income.

This book is meant to be brief and get the point across. It is packed with useful information and plenty of examples to demonstrate why the techniques work. It is my desire to share with you what I've learned and the HELOC model that I've created from my journey. A mortgage, be it simple interest or variable interest, is all math. Once you understand the math concept behind it, the rest is easy to apply.

You do not need to have a mathematics degree to use the method. This book is all you need. There is no fee-based program for you to join, either. To get the most out of this book, I suggest you follow the Recommended Actions at the end of each chapter. You can use the template provided here or create your own.

It is truly an exhilarating feeling to see your mortgage balance decreasing rapidly with each statement you receive from the lender and seeing the total interest you're saving. I hope you will apply the techniques from this book and reap the rewards.

## CHAPTER 1

GETTING STARTED

Because you are reading this book, you are a homeowner and want to pay off your mortgage sooner. Or you are a renter but plan to buy a home soon and want to know how to accelerate your mortgage payoff.

There are many options. The most common ones are paying extra principal each month, making a few extra payments each year, or enroll in a bi-weekly payment schedule. In this book, I'd like you to explore the unconventional method, using HELOC toward your advantage.

The concept of HELOC is not new. There are a variety of reasons why people want to access HELOC. The process is relatively easy. My former manager tapped into his HELOC to help pay for his children's college. Some say that is not a wise choice, but others disagree. Another one of my colleagues opened a HELOC just to have it ready for use. He didn't need any money, but he wanted that line of credit for security reasons. Since there is zero cost associated with opening a HELOC, he had one set up just in case he needed to use it. There is no right or wrong reason. It all depends on your particular situation.

The most common reason that homeowners open a HELOC is to use it for home renovation. This includes updating an older home or upgrading kitchen/bath before putting the house on the market for sale, hoping to gain a greater return. Then there are some people who tap into their HELOC to pay for an expensive vacation. That is a foolish decision, in my opinion, and I discourage you from doing so. If you cannot afford to pay for your vacation with the residual income, then take a less-extravagant trip or do a "staycation." Staycations are becoming more common. It is great for families with young children, more relaxing for the parents, and less hassle for the kids. Tapping into your house's equity to pay for a vacation has greater risk in the event that you cannot repay the loan. The lender can foreclose on your home.

Perhaps the *one* method that the majority of people have *not* tried to use HELOC for is to accelerate their mortgage payoff. You may have heard of it but never really understood the mechanics of it. Or you wonder whether it is even possible and are more than a little skeptical about it. After all, your mortgage-interest rate is fixed and may be lower than the HELOC rate, which is variable. You have been told to stay away from variable interest rates. Because of this, you automatically ruled it out. As you will see in the following chapters, this is a myth due to lack of understanding. The math will prove this otherwise.

In life, we tend to be afraid when we don't understand something. When we are afraid, we hesitate to make a decision. When we don't make a decision, we fail to take action. When we fail to take action, we miss out on life's opportunities. My goal is to unravel the math of HELOC and any misperceptions people have about it. Then, you can follow the steps in this book and make smart decisions. This book will show you the possibilities of a HELOC and the benefits of using it to pay off your mortgage expeditiously faster.

CHAPTER 2

THE FUNDAMENTALS OF INTEREST RATES

I presume you have some knowledge about what a HELOC is. If you do not know, it is worthwhile to spend a few minutes reading the booklet "What you should know about home equity lines of credit," issued by the Consumer Financial Protection Bureau (CFPB). You can also visit your bank's website to read about it. This helps when you apply for the HELOC loan.

Fundamentally, unlike a conventional mortgage, HELOC is *not* a fixed interest rate. The rate varies according to the Prime Rate, which is based on the Federal Fund Rate, set by the Federal Reserve. Rates can change monthly. Your rate will be determined by your bank, based on your personal credit history.

It is important to clarify some basic differences between the standard mortgage interest calculation and the HELOC interest calculations. This is the crux of leveraging a HELOC to pay off a mortgage early.

Inherently, both types of loans are simple-interest-accrual, except that one is calculated based on daily balance and the other one is based on monthly balance. Once you understand the basics, you will be able to follow the logic and refute the myth and those who try to discourage you from using a HELOC.

HELOC Interest Calculation

The HELOC interest is calculated based on the daily balance. This interest rate is variable, and it changes when the Prime Rate changes. The Prime Rate is tied to the Federal Reserve Bank.

Formula: *Interest = (Interest rate ÷ 365 days) x (loan balance) x (# days accrued interest)*

$$\underbrace{}_{\text{DAILY INTEREST}}$$

Example:

Loan Amount = $5,000
Interest Rate = 5% variable

Using the formula above, you can calculate the interest:
i = (5% ÷ 365) x $5,000 x 31
= 0.000137 x $5,000 x 31
= $21.23

In a month with 31 days, you would have owed $21.23 if you waited until the last day of the month to repay. Now, let's assume you received your paycheck twice a month, and you were able to repay $500 on the 10th day and another $100 on the 28th day. The interest is recalculated each time a repayment is made.

Let's break this down. For a payment made on the 10th day against an outstanding balance of $5,000, you have to pay interest only from the first day to the 9th day, a total of 9 days. Therefore, the total interest = $6.16

$i = (5\% \div 365) \times \$5,000 \times 9\ days$
$= \$6.16$

For the remainder of the balance of $4,500, you then made another payment on the 28th day, paying interest from the 10th to the 27th, a total of 18 days. Total interest for the period = $11.10

$i = (5\% \div 365) \times \$4,500 \times 18\ days$
$= \$11.10$

Between the two repayments, your total interest is $19.67. You can see the difference between $21.23 if you waited until the last day of the month to repay vs. $19.67 if you repaid on two different occasions within that month. The interest calculation continues each time a repayment is made until the entire balance is paid off. If you draw from a HELOC before repaying the entire amount, the interest gets recalculated based on the new daily balance.

For those of you who are Microsoft Excel gurus, you can set this up easily in Excel as shown in *Figure 2–1* and project how much interest you owe with different payment amounts. You are not required to use Excel. In this simple-interest loan, the key is to make payments as often as you can, to reduce the total interest.

DATE	DRAW	PAYMENT	BALANCE	INTEREST
3/1			$5,000.00	$0.68
3/2			$5,000.00	$0.68
3/3			$5,000.00	$0.68
3/4			$5,000.00	$0.68
3/5			$5,000.00	$0.68
3/6			$5,000.00	$0.68
3/7			$5,000.00	$0.68

DATE	DRAW	PAYMENT	BALANCE	INTEREST
3/8			$5,000.00	$0.68
3/9			$5,000.00	$0.68
3/10		$500.00	$4,500.00	$0.62
3/11			$4,500.00	$0.62
3/12			$4,500.00	$0.62
3/13			$4,500.00	$0.62
3/14			$4,500.00	$0.62
3/15			$4,500.00	$0.62
3/16			$4,500.00	$0.62
3/17			$4,500.00	$0.62
3/18			$4,500.00	$0.62
3/19			$4,500.00	$0.62
3/20			$4,500.00	$0.62
3/21			$4,500.00	$0.62
3/22			$4,500.00	$0.62
3/23			$4,500.00	$0.62
3/24			$4,500.00	$0.62
3/25			$4,500.00	$0.62
3/26			$4,500.00	$0.62
3/27			$4,500.00	$0.62
3/28		$100.00	$4,400.00	$0.60
3/29			$4,400.00	$0.60
3/30			$4,400.00	$0.60
3/31			$4,400.00	$0.60
TOTAL	$0.00	$600.00		$19.67

FIGURE 2-1: Simple interest on a $5,000 loan at 5% interest repaid twice

Because a HELOC has a variable interest rate, the 5% interest rate used in the example above can change to 4% one month or 6%, depending on the Prime Rate. In that case, you adjust the interest factor in the formula and follow the same calculation. In a later chapter, I will show you that, even at a higher variable interest rate, the result is still more favorable than a lower, fixed mortgage rate.

Standard Mortgage Interest

The standard mortgage interest is calculated monthly, based on the outstanding loan balance. The interest rate is fixed. The interest amount remains the same within the month whether you made payment on the first or the fifteenth of that month.

Formula: *Interest = (Interest rate ÷ 12 months) x (loan balance)*

$$\underbrace{\hspace{4cm}}_{\text{MONTHLY INTEREST}}$$

Example:
    House Cost = $350,000
    Down Payment = $70,000 (20% down)
    Mortgage = $280,000
    Interest Rate = 5% fixed
    Term = 30 years

Interest is calculated as follows:
    i = (5% ÷ 12) x loan balance
    = 0.004167x $280,000
    = $1,166.67

Your monthly payment stays the same. The interest will decrease over time as principal increases. At the end of 30 years, you have paid $261,116 worth of interest, almost enough to buy another house. Due to space constraint, the amortization schedule in *Figure 2–2* is truncated to show only the first 12 months of the payments.

| 1st Year Total | $18,037.21 | $13,906.18 | $4,131.02 | |
| 30 Years Total | $541,116.20 | $261,116.20 | $280,000.00 | |
MONTH	PAYMENT	INTEREST	PRINCIPAL	ENDING BALANCE
1	$1,503.10	$1,166.67	$336.43	$279,663.57
2	$1,503.10	$1,165.26	$337.84	$279,325.73
3	$1,503.10	$1,163.86	$339.24	$278,986.49
4	$1,503.10	$1,162.44	$340.66	$278,645.83
5	$1,503.10	$1,161.02	$342.08	$278,303.75
6	$1,503.10	$1,159.60	$343.50	$277,960.25
7	$1,503.10	$1,158.17	$344.93	$277,615.32
8	$1,503.10	$1,156.73	$346.37	$277,268.95
9	$1,503.10	$1,155.29	$347.81	$276,921.14
10	$1,503.10	$1,153.84	$349.26	$276,571.87
11	$1,503.10	$1,152.38	$350.72	$276,221.16
12	$1,503.10	$1,150.92	$352.18	$275,868.98

FIGURE 2-2: First-year amortization schedule for $350,000 loan at 5% interest with 20% down

It is important to understand the distinction between these two types of interest calculations, as it builds the foundation for the upcoming chapters.

For those who are interested in setting this up in Excel, I have included the template and formulas in *Appendix A*.

Recommended Actions:
1. Review the interest calculation.
2. Understand the concept of the two types of interest accrual, daily vs. monthly.
3. Optional: Practice the formula using various balances, interest rates, and interest amounts.

CHAPTER 3

YOUR FINANCES

Those of you who have experience with performing physical inventory in manufacturing or retail understand how daunting this task can be. No one enjoys it, but if it's done on a regular basis, the upkeep is minimum. Physical inventory is crucial to the business operations and management for reasons other than meeting IRS requirements. After all, the paper record should match the physical counts. Otherwise, how do you know when to restock or to offload the excess? How accurate is your system if you don't track or reconcile records?

Your personal finances are the same. If you haven't already, at a minimum, you ought to track your household income and expenses. Otherwise, how do you know what you have or don't have? You need to know your financial health picture. If your expenses exceed your income month after month, the techniques describe in this book will not work for you. Management consultant Peter Drucker once said, "What gets measured gets improved." It truly does. This chapter focuses on taking your own financial inventory at the simplest level possible.

Tracking System

To begin, you should develop a method to track your cash flow. It is important to know what is coming in and what is going out. While you develop this habit, you will start to see where your money goes and will be able to redirect it instead of living from paycheck to paycheck.

This system does not need to be complicated, and you do not need a computer. Paper and pen will get the job done. In my college days, when I didn't own a personal computer, I used the school equipment to set up a simple Excel template and print out pages on which I would write the month and dates, one page per month. I then stapled all of the pages together and recorded all of my expenses. If I spent $5 on a specific date of the month, I recorded that amount on the paper. With income from my part-time work-study and the expenses going out to pay for rent, food, movies, etc., I tallied it all up at month's end and saw how much surplus or shortage I had. It also allowed me to plan for the next month.

To this day, I maintain this habit—but now I keep it on my laptop instead of printing hard copies. You can create your own or use the template in *Figure 3–1*. This is what I currently use for my personal expense tracking, one for each month. You can customize it to your own circumstances and make it as detailed or as simple as you want. Keep in mind that you do have to maintain this. Therefore, striking a balance is important. You will be less likely to keep it up to date if you make it too complicated or difficult to maintain.

DATE	GROCERY	AUTO/GAS	DINE OUT/ ENTERTAIN- MENT	CLOTHING	HOUSEHOLD SUPPLIES	SCHOOL/ SPORT ACTIVITIES	MISC	TOTAL
1/1								
1/2								
1/3								
1/4								
1/5								
1/6								
1/7								
1/8								
1/9								
1/10								
1/11								
1/12								
1/13								
1/14								
1/15								
1/16								
1/17								
1/18								
1/19								
1/20								
1/21								
1/22								
1/23								
1/24								
1/25								
1/26								
1/27								
1/28								
1/29								
1/30								
1/31								
TOTAL								

FIGURE 3-1: Monthly Expense Tracking Template

The categories in the template are loosely defined. There isn't a right or wrong way to do it, as long as you are consistent with the grouping. For example, if you buy cleaning products from the grocery store, those expenses are all in the same receipt for produce and other foods. You can enter that into the "Grocery" category, or you can segregate that amount and enter it into the "Household" category. Whichever method you use, make sure you are consistent with it so that it is properly recorded regularly. The main point is that you are developing a habit to track your cash flow. Here are some guidelines to help you group your expenses.

- ✓ *Groceries*—Food that you buy from the supermarket.
- ✓ *Auto/Gas*—Gas that you put into your vehicles. Also includes tolls or repair expenses.
- ✓ *Dine Out/Entertainment*—Eating out, ordering out, movies, concerts, or shows.
- ✓ *Clothing*—Clothes, shoes, all apparel.
- ✓ *Household Supplies*—Cleaning products and supplies, toiletries, laundry products—anything that keeps the household running.
- ✓ *School/Sport Activities*—School field-trip fee, school lunches, kids' sports registration fee—any funds that you use to pay for school-related activities.
- ✓ *Miscellaneous*—Everything else can be recorded here. For example, birthday gifts, Christmas gifts, unexpected medical bills, etc.—items that are one time only, non-recurring.

If tracking your expenses is new to you, give yourself some time to adjust. First, take a blank envelope, and mark "Receipts" on the front. Each time you purchase something, take the receipt, and put it into the envelope for data entry later on. For example, if you purchased a $20 birthday gift for your friend, keep that receipt, and put it in an envelope when you get home. If you just took your family out for a dinner, keep that receipt, and put it into the envelope along with all other receipts. If you contributed to a charity with your credit card, and they did not print you a receipt, write it down on a sticky note, your smartphone, on a napkin, or whatever, and put it into the envelope. If you ordered something from Amazon, write it down, and put it into the envelope. It takes discipline, but it will pay off.

The monthly expense tally provides you a micro-level of where your money goes day to day. It will also reveal how frequently you make trips to stores. For example, one year, I noticed that I stopped at the grocery store fifteen times in November! That was excessive! It was not efficient, and it was a waste of time and gas. I wouldn't have known that without seeing it on paper. It changed my behavior to plan ahead prior to venturing out. Your example could be dining out fifteen times a month and, therefore, an opportunity to reduce it in order to save some money.

Tracking it on paper, you now can see how much you spend and where are you spending the most and the least. If you ever need to cut back, you'll know which categories you can do that in.

In addition to the day-to-day or monthly level, you want to understand the whole picture at the macro level, an aggregate, yearly view. This is achieved simply by adding the monthly totals. If it's done in Excel, you can set the data to be automatically carried over from the monthly entry into the yearly entry. Manual addition isn't all that bad, either. Monthly bills, such as utilities, water and sewer fees, mortgage, or condo fees should be entered as well. See *Figure 3–2.*

CATEGORIES	JAN	FEB	MAR	APR	MAY	JUN	JUL	AUG	SEP	OCT	NOV	DEC	TOTAL
INCOME													
EXPENSES:													
PITI:													
Principal													
Interest													
Escrow													
Property Tax													
Insurance													
PMI													
HELOC Interest													
Utilities:													
Phone													
Electric													
Propane													
Water													
Sewer													
Grocery													
Auto/Gas													
Dining Out													
Clothing													
Household													
School													
Misc													
Auto Insurance													
Professional Fee													
TOTAL EXPENSES													
NET													

FIGURE 3-2: Aggregate Yearly Expense Template

Guidelines to help you formulate the table:

✓ *Income*—Net pay from your job. The key word here is *net*, which is your take-home pay after all deductions and taxes are taken from the paycheck. Make sure to include any dividends or stocks that you receive on a monthly basis in this field also.

✓ *Expenses*—There are various categories here. Some are broken down into greater detail.

PITI (1)—Principal, Interest, Tax, Insurance. Most likely your property tax is escrowed by the lender unless you pay it on our own. Enter the property tax in either the "Escrow" or "Property Tax" field, not both. If you do not own a house, change this to "rent," and record your monthly rent amount. Private Mortgage Insurance (PMI) is only applicable if you took out a FHA loan with less than 20% down. PMI is itemized on your statement from the lender.

✓ *HELOC Interest*—Once you begin to use a HELOC to accelerate the mortgage repayment, the interest incurred is an expense and should be captured here.

✓ *Utilities*: (2)—If you still have a landline for phone in addition to a cell phone, add both bills here. Depending on what you use for fuel, change it to reflect yours. I used propane; yours could be oil or natural gas. Add water and sewer fee. Some towns may charge you these fees only on a quarterly basis instead of monthly. If so, divide it by three.

✓ *Grocery . . . Misc.* (3)—These are what you recorded in *Figure 3–1*. You can set Excel to carry the numbers over automatically. Or do it the old-fashioned way—pen, paper, and a calculator.

✓ *Auto Insurance*—Premium for auto insurance over a twelve-month period. If you pay a lump sum annually, spread it equally across twelve months. Likewise, if you pay semi-annually, spread it over six months.

✓ *Professional Fees*—This is for occasionally used professionals such as accountant, legal, land survey, plumber, or others.

Add up all of the expenses.

With income and expense entered, the net is the residual income (Net = Income—Total Expenses). If the net is a positive number, congratulations: you have extra money left over after all expenses are paid. If the net is a negative number, you may want to review the spending on each category and cut back. You have a choice to bring in additional sources of income to sustain your current lifestyle or change your lifestyle to align with your current income.

VERY IMPORTANT: For the techniques in this book to work, your net income MUST be positive!

Data Entry Frequency

Recording the spending should not be a time-consuming exercise. To increase efficiency, I recommend entering the spending information twice a month. There is an advantage in doing this twice a month as opposed to once a month. This method provides you a rearview mirror look of what you have spent in the first half of the month and gives you flexibility on how you want to curtail your second half of the month spending. It can prevent you from having a negative cash flow. Once you have established the routine, you can update it once a month.

The benefit to this tracking system is that you know exactly how much is coming in, how much is going out, and where it is going to.

Before the end of each month, you can predict whether you will have a surplus or a shortage. It allows you to plan ahead. Month after month, you have control of your hard-earned money. If there is residual income, you have choices—to use it for a vacation, pay off the house, or take some time off from work. Likewise, if your outflow is more than your inflow, the tracking gives you an accurate picture of how "bad" the gap is. It is also simple to do.

One caution here is "DO NOT COUNT THE MONEY BEFORE YOU RECEIVE IT." For example, don't count on a tax refund until the money is in your bank account. Don't count on that bonus until you receive it. Don't count on the pay increase until you see it reflected in your paycheck.

Know Your Finances

The more knowledgeable you are about your own financial situation, the better equipped you are. Armed with the details about your financial health, you can be confident with what you can afford before a lender presents you with a monthly payment plan or approves you for a loan. Lenders follow general lending guidelines; they do not know your financial situation intimately like you do. You can also sleep better at night knowing your own numbers.

If you don't go through the exercise above or maintain the habit of knowing your cash-flow position, you are leaving your finances in someone else's hands, someone who has no stake in your long-term financial well-being. You can use the lender to help you, but you are accountable and responsible for your own future. Take control of your own finances.

Whether you are a man or woman, a good analogy I'd like to use to emphasize this point is when you go to a shoe store. You are greeted by a friendly shoe salesman. You explain to him the type of shoes, brand, color, size, and the price range you want to pay. A few moments later, he brings back a few choices for you to try. Only you know how it fits and feels. The shoe salesman does not know. He brings shoes that fit your general description. It is completely up to you to decide what is good for you. The same concept applies to your finances.

If you have been living from paycheck to paycheck, I strongly urge you to begin tracking your cash flow using the above templates. In a few months, I guarantee that you will become a better manager of your money.

Recommended Actions:
1. Gather your existing receipts and put them into an envelope.
2. Set up the income and expense tracking using the template provided in this chapter, or create your own.
3. Record all expenses and income at least once a month.
4. Review where the money is going on a monthly basis.
5. Decide what to do with the residual income (more on this in a later chapter).

CHAPTER 4

PITI

While the primary goal of this book is to show you how to pay off your mortgage sooner, it is equally important to keep the cost of homeownership as low as possible. This chapter offers some practical tips to help you do that. Every month you write a check to the lender; that total amount includes Principal, Interest, Property Tax, and Home Insurance, also referred to as "PITI" by lenders. If you put less than 20% down payment, you are responsible for paying PMI.

Lenders are required to escrow property tax through the monthly payment from homeowners. They review, analyze, and project the escrow annually to ensure that there are sufficient funds to cover the tax bill from your municipality when due. If the projection shows a surplus, they will mail you the excess in a check. If the projection shows a shortage, you have the option of sending them a lump sum for the shortage amount or amortizing it into your monthly payment. This is a personal choice. I typically let them amortize the amount into my monthly payment.

The lender will continue to collect your property tax as part of the monthly payment and pay your city or town tax collector on your behalf when it is due; it is a sure way to prevent the municipality from placing a tax lien on the property. Remember, you don't own the property until you've paid it off. The lender holds the title until then. Therefore, they made sure the property tax payment is current.

Depending on the balance of your mortgage and whether you have a good payment history with the lender, you may be able to remove the property tax from the monthly payment and pay it directly to your municipality. This practice varies from lender to lender. Verify with your lender first.

I did so with Wells Fargo on my first townhouse. Upon my request to remove the tax from being escrowed, they reviewed my loan balance and payment history, and allowed me to pay the property tax directly to my town. In their view, I was a low risk for being delinquent in paying the tax bill.

Why would anyone want to do that? After all, the tax bill can be hefty to pay all at once. I do it to have more control over where my money goes. The total PITI for a given year may not change, but the month-to-month movement of the cash does. For this reason, I use it as leverage to meet some of the short-term needs. If you are going to do this, make sure you budget the money for the tax and are able to pay for it when it comes due. The lender collects more than the actual tax-bill amount from the homeowners for a cushion in anticipation of the tax increase. It is legal. As a homeowner, I want that extra money in my possession instead of sending it to the lender.

Let's look at the example below:

	SCENARIO 1	SCENARIO 2
Principal =	$1,300	$1,300
Interest =	$730	$730
Tax =	$800	
Insurance =	Assumed Paid	
Total Monthly =	$2,830	$2,030

FIGURE 4–1: Monthly PITI

Scenario 1—Property tax is escrowed by the lender as part of the monthly bill.

Scenario 2— Property tax is not escrowed. Homeowner pays the tax bill directly to their town/city during billing cycle.

In Scenario 2, by keeping the $800 tax each month, the homeowner can use this money to pay for deferred repairs, replacing appliances, or for unexpected medical expenses. Having cash means having flexibility. With that said, the homeowner must be absolutely sure that there is enough money to cover the large, lump-sum $4,800 ($800 x 6 months) for a semi-annual tax bill. This is where your financial tracking system comes in handy.

Lowering Your Property Tax

If you noticed that your property tax seemed high, please do take a look at the taxes of other properties around your neighborhood. It is not difficult to do as this information is available to the public. Each town or city has a website that can be accessed from your own home or from the town office to review this data.

If you feel you are being taxed higher than your surrounding neighbors with similar homes, you can make a case and appeal to your city assessor's office. Each town and city has its own rules and regulations governing the abatement process. This process is valuable, and I encourage you to become familiar with it. It is absolutely possible for homeowners to reduce their property tax when the appeal is successful. I have done so myself.

Unlike the mortgage, where the loan amount is finite and you can pay it off, the property tax bill is guaranteed for life. We can expect the property tax only to increase over time as the real-estate value increases. Therefore, keeping your property tax bill low is just as important as accelerating your mortgage payoff. It is in every homeowner's best interest to monitor their tax bill and appeal it if it's out of line with other, similar properties in the surrounding areas.

Appealing Elements

Suppose you find your tax bill is high, and you want to appeal it. What do you need? Your town/city has an abatement form that you can fill out. To increase your probability of success, I highly recommend that you include some objective evidence to justify your appeal. Any one of the following documents will suffice:

1. *Comparative Market Analysis* (CMA)—Similar to what realtors provide to a seller prior to listing the house on the Multiple Listing System (MLS). They pull a list of recently sold properties, similar to yours, and suggest a reasonable price. You can look up tax cards of similar houses and compare the basic characteristics, such as lot acreage, number of bedrooms, number of baths, and square footage. Then focus on the property tax value, and determine the "should be" value for your property tax. This is the value you should aim to achieve from the appeal. If you have access to a realtor, ask them to pull the CMA for you.
2. *Appraisal*—This is another alternative if you recently bought your house or if you decided to pay a few hundred dollars for an independent professional to appraise your house. You'll want to include a copy of the appraisal report along with the completed appeal form justifying what your property-tax bill should be.

Once you have completed the appeal package, make sure to adhere to the submission deadline and retain a copy for yourself. After you submit it, you can expect one of two things to happen.

1. Your town/city may pay you a personal visit to assess the interior and exterior of your house. That assessor may even come equipped with notepad and measuring tape to record during the walk-through. You absolutely have the right to refuse, but know that, if you do not cooperate, your appeal may be denied. In my case, I let the assessor in, accompanied him during the walk-through, and asked him to be respectful of my personal items. I had a town assessor who was nosy. He opened all closets and cabinets even though they bore no value in his assessment. Setting expectations with the assessor on the time limit spent inside of your house will help, too.

2. The other thing that could happen is that your town/city may conduct a "desk audit" by reviewing your appeal on paper instead of sending an inspector out to the site. This could occur in a town/city that is densely populated with home ownership, making on-site assessment neither cost effective nor, sometimes, even possible.

It took me a couple of weekends to complete the abatement application. Three months later, I received a partial refund in the mail. It was absolutely worth the effort.

While trying to lower the property-tax bill may sound enticing, there needs to be a balance. The property tax is calculated based on your assessed value. An extremely low property tax implies that your house value is also low. This could place you at a disadvantage if you had to sell your house under less-than-desirable circumstances. It is also important to distinguish the difference between the assessed value and the market value. They are not always the same.

The assessed value is determined by your town. It is then multiplied by the tax rate to set the property-tax value. The market value is determined by the real-estate market in your local area. Thus, realtors use MLS to pull comparables to determine the reasonable price. The assessed value is not equal to the market value. They can go in either direction.

Recommended Actions:

1. Review your tax bill.
2. Look up the property-tax value of "similar to" homes in your area, and compare it to yours.
3. If you feel your property is over-assessed, get familiar with your town's abatement process, forms, and procedures.
4. Appeal by following the steps described in this chapter.

## CHAPTER 5

SECURING A HELOC

As I mentioned before, each chapter builds on the previous foundation. So far, you have learned the key difference between the HELOC interest vs. the standard mortgage interest and can accurately estimate how much interest you will incur, given any loan amount, interest rate, and down payment. You also understand why it is important to track your financial health. Additionally, you've learned how to lower your property tax bill if it is unreasonably high. All of these steps are to prepare you for paying off your mortgage quicker. You are ready to set up a HELOC and tap into it, but how do you go about securing one? What should you be looking for? This chapter will show you what questions to ask and what should you avoid.

Obviously, no lender will approve you for a HELOC if there is no equity in your home. How much equity your home has depends on how much you put down or how long you've been making payments. If you just closed a home and put 20% as a down payment, that's 20% instant equity. If you put more than 20% down, you have more than 20% equity. Those who have a Federal Housing Administration (FHA) loan and pay only the minimum down payment of 3.5%, you have 3.5% equity.

While you're shopping for a HELOC, below are the minimum criteria. You can also use a list of questions in *Figure 5–1* to evaluate each lender's product.

HELOC Criteria

1. Zero dollar ($0) for application fee.
2. Zero dollar ($0) for appraisal fee—the lender still has to appraise your home in order to determine your home's value and the amount that you can borrow. Make sure you request a copy of the appraisal report. If your home is assessed over and above the appraised value, you can use this report for your property-tax abatement process as described in the previous chapter.
3. Zero dollar ($0) for closing fee—the lender will absorb it. You may have to pay $50-$100 for a record fee, depending on what your local Registry of Deeds charges. It should be minimum.
4. Interest payment only—Option to pay interest only if available. This is good for a real-estate investor who wants the minimum monthly payment. It is not a deal-breaker if they don't offer this option.
5. A HELOC used as a checking account—There is a huge advantage to this, but don't be surprised if your bank does not allow it or their system cannot support it.

When the HELOC and the checking account are one and the same, bill-paying management is easier. You eliminate the hassle of transferring funds between the two accounts to avoid overdrafts. More importantly, it reduces the interest, as HELOC interest is calculated based on daily balance. This means that, whenever money goes into the HELOC account, the interest is recalculated that day.

Selecting a bank with either no minimum-balance requirement or a very low minimum-balance requirement is the best choice. In other words, it is preferable to choose a bank that requires you to maintain an account minimum balance of only $100 vs. $1,000. I stay away from the banks requiring more than $100 minimum balance. Don't overlook your local credit unions; they are usually very competitive and have the lowest account minimum-balance requirement.

	QUESTIONS	ANSWERS		
		LENDER A	LENDER B	LENDER C
1	What is your repayment policy?			
2	Do you have a product that is interest repayment only?			
3	How much of a discount will I get if I become a member of your bank?			
4	How long does it take to get approved?			
5	Do you allow HELOC to be used as a checking account that can receive direct deposits and online bill paying?			
6	Are there fees that I have to pay?			

FIGURE 5–1: Qualifying Questions for HELOC Lenders

I made a mistake of not doing my due diligence upfront when I was applying for a HELOC. I chose my bank for convenience. As a result, my HELOC lacked the checking account features that would have been more beneficial. It worked out at the end but it required a lot of self-discipline to maintain the two accounts transactions.

HELOC is a popular loan. The approval process takes anywhere from 2-8 weeks. It depends on the current market interest rate and the volume of applicants. Plan accordingly.

Recommended Actions:
1. Get referrals from people who have used a HELOC.
2. Select 2–3 lenders or banks to interview/evaluate.
3. Select one lender/bank and move forward with the application.

CHAPTER 6

SKEPTICISM VS. PROOF

Some of you reading this book are still skeptical about how a HELOC can really help and whether it is better than some of the more-well-known methods, such as sending extra payments. We are going to walk through an example to prove it.

Suppose you are a new homeowner who just closed on your house, with the following terms.

Example:

- ✓ House = $350,000
- ✓ Down Payment = 5% (or $17,500). This is also the equity.
- ✓ Mortgage balance = $332,500
- ✓ Interest rate = 4.0% fixed
- ✓ Term = 30 years
- ✓ Monthly Payment = $1,587.41

PMI is intentionally left out of this analysis, as it has no bearing on the interest. The first year of the amortization schedule is in *Figure 6–1:*

1st Year Total	$19,048.87	$13,193.42	$5,855.45	
30 Years Total	$571,466.11	$238,966.11	$332,500.00	
MONTH	**PAYMENT**	**INTEREST**	**PRINCIPAL**	**ENDING BALANCE**
1	$1,587.41	$1,108.33	$479.07	$332,020.93
2	$1,587.41	$1,106.74	$480.67	$331,540.26
3	$1,587.41	$1,105.13	$482.27	$331,057.99
4	$1,587.41	$1,103.53	$483.88	$330,574.11
5	$1,587.41	$1,101.91	$485.49	$330,088.61
6	$1,587.41	$1,100.30	$487.11	$329,601.50
7	$1,587.41	$1,098.67	$488.73	$329,112.77
8	$1,587.41	$1,097.04	$490.36	$328,622.41
9	$1,587.41	$1,095.41	$492.00	$328,130.41
10	$1,587.41	$1,093.77	$493.64	$327,636.77
11	$1,587.41	$1,092.12	$495.28	$327,141.49
12	$1,587.41	$1,090.47	$496.93	$326,644.55

FIGURE 6–1: First 12 months' amortization schedule

Your total payment is $19,048 at the end of the first year, of which 69% ($13,193.42) is interest and only 31% ($5,855.45) is principal. If you stay on this schedule and continue to pay without modifying your payment amount, you will have paid a total of $571,466 at the end of 30 years for a $350,000 house.

Suppose you have access to $2,000 to put it toward the principal in the 3rd month. Let's see how much you can save on interest and how many years you can shave off the loan with this one-time lump-sum transaction. See *Figure 6-2* and *Figure 6-3.*

	PAYMENT	INTEREST	PRINCIPAL	ENDING BALANCE	LUMP-SUM
1st Year Total	$19,048.87	$13,132.62	$7,916.25		
29.7 Years Total	$564,939.14	$234,439.14	$332,500.00		$2,000.00
MONTH	PAYMENT	INTEREST	PRINCIPAL	ENDING BALANCE	LUMP-SUM
1	$1,587.41	$1,108.33	$479.07	$332,020.93	
2	$1,587.41	$1,106.74	$480.67	$331,540.26	
3	$1,587.41	$1,105.13	$2,482.27	$329,057.99	$2,000.00
4	$1,587.41	$1,096.86	$490.55	$328,567.44	
5	$1,587.41	$1,095.22	$492.18	$328,075.26	
6	$1,587.41	$1,093.58	$493.82	$327,581.44	
7	$1,587.41	$1,091.94	$495.47	$327,085.97	
8	$1,587.41	$1,090.29	$497.12	$326,588.85	
9	$1,587.41	$1,088.63	$498.78	$326,090.07	
10	$1,587.41	$1,086.97	$500.44	$325,589.64	
11	$1,587.41	$1,085.30	$502.11	$325,087.53	
12	$1,587.41	$1,083.63	$503.78	$324,583.75	

FIGURE 6–2: First 12 months of amortization with one lump-sum $2,000 extra principal payment

You would have saved $4,527 in interest and paid off 4 months earlier!

PAYMENT OPTION	TOTAL PAYMENT	TOTAL INTEREST PAID	Paid Off	
			MONTH	YEAR
No Extra Payment	$571,466	$238,966	360	30
One-time $2,000	$564,939	$234,439	356	29.7
Difference	$6,527	$4,527	4	0.3

FIGURE 6–3: Interest saved when paid $2,000 lump-sum payment

The Excel template and formulas for this calculation are in *Appendix B*. You would see that your last payment is in month 356, a four months reduction with a single lump-sum principal payment. Imagine if you continue to do this every few months? How much quicker can you pay off your mortgage?

The above is just one example and one proof. The next chapter will show you additional examples and analysis of what happens if you apply this method on multiple occasions.

Recommended Actions:
1. If you are an Excel user, practice setting up the model following the instructions in Appendix B.

## CHAPTER 7

COMPARATIVE ANALYSIS: EXTRA PRINCIPAL PAYMENTS VS. HELOC PAYMENTS

To provide *quantitative analysis* and compare various payment options, this chapter is slightly more technical and has heavier math content than previous chapters. It is not necessary that you know the math or follow it. It is more important for you to understand the techniques than be able to do the math. Your lender will do the math for you when they send in the monthly statement and Form-1099 at year's end. It captures the interest and principal amount you paid.

To reiterate, one absolute requirement for the techniques described here to work is that your net income must be positive. You must have more income coming in than expenses going out every month. Otherwise, the model will not work.

Whether it is a 15- or 30-year mortgage, we know that interests are front-end loaded. As principal is paid down, the interest decreases, and the principal will eventually exceed the interest. An example of this is shown in *Figure 7–1* for a $332,500 mortgage at 4% fixed interest rate over 30 years. The principal in the graph begins to exceed the interest on the 153rd payment or month assuming no extra payments were made—that's about 12.75 years into the loan. It is a long time!

360 months Amortization

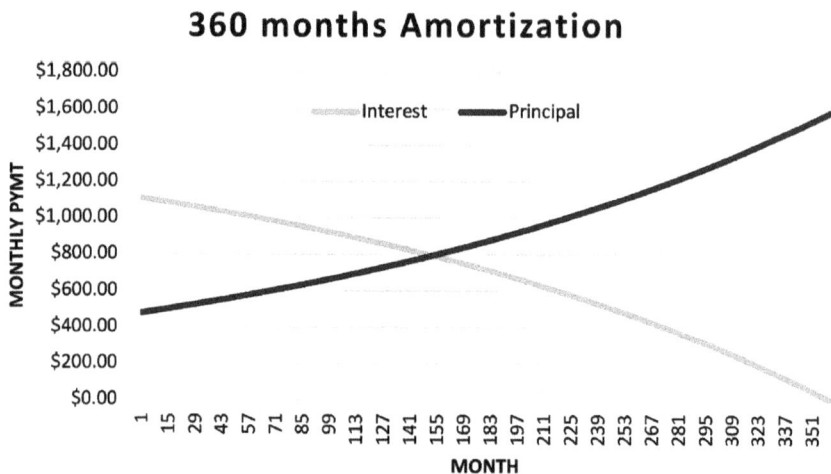

FIGURE 7–1: Principal and interest over 360 months

The good news is that you can influence this. You saw the impact that a single principal payment has on the total interest and how it reduced the loan term in the last chapter. With just $2,000, you saved $4,527 in interest and shaved off 4 months.

It is safe to assume that there aren't many homeowners who consistently have thousands of dollars of residual income at month's end, after all bills are paid. Therefore, it is unrealistic to expect a homeowner to pay thousands of extra dollars toward principal month after month. So then, what do you do? This is where a HELOC comes into play.

Suppose you have access to this kind of money every few months. How will that look? Using the same scenario as in Chapter 6, if you paid $2,000 in month 3, another in month 7, and another in month 12, with no additional principal afterward, you would have saved a total of $13,050 interest and would pay off your home in 29 years. See *Figure 7–2* for summary.

HELOC Method			Paid Off			
MONTH	LUMP-SUM AMOUNT	TOTAL INTEREST PAID	MONTH	YEAR	TOTAL EXTRA PMT	INTEREST SAVED
3, 7, 12	$2,000	$225,916	348	29.0	$6,000	$13,050

FIGURE 7—2: Reduced one year in mortgage and saved $13,050 interest using lump-sum payment on three occasions

The set-up is the same as in *Appendix B*. For the additional lump-sum principal payments, add the amount to the corresponding month, and then compare the interest to the total interest if there wasn't any additional principal payment. Again, you are not expected to be a mathematician. The takeaway here is to look at how much interest is saved and number of years the loan is reduced with each lump-sum payment.

To take the above example a little further, suppose you continue with this rhythm. If you apply $2,000 to fourteen random months, totaling $28,000 extra principal, you would have saved more than $49,000 interest and reduced the term from 30 years to 26 years. See *Figure 7-3*. This is how homeowners can leverage a HELOC to pay off a mortgage at an accelerated pace.

HELOC Method			Paid Off			
MONTH	LUMP-SUM AMOUNT	TOTAL INTEREST PAID	MONTH	YEAR	TOTAL EXTRA PMT	INTEREST SAVED
3, 7, 12, 15, 18, 23, 27, 31, 37, 42, 46, 48, 53, 57	$2,000	$189,376	312	26.0	$28,000	$49,590

FIGURE 7—3: Reduced mortgage term by four years and saved more than $49,000 in interest with lump-sum payment on various occasions.

The next section will walk you through the comparison of traditional vs. HELOC approaches and the result of "what if" examples using Scenario 1 below. Regardless of the method you use, keep in mind that, in addition to the extra principal, you are still required to make the regular monthly payment to the lender. PMI is required when putting less than 20% down, but, for the examples in this chapter, we will not include PMI in the analysis. You just have to know that, the sooner you build equity, the quicker you can remove PMI.

Scenario 1: New homeowner:
    Home Price = $350,000
    Down Payment = $17,500 (5%)
    Mortgage = $332,500
    Term = 30 years
    Interest rate = 4% fixed

Traditional Method—Paying Extra Principal Monthly

The traditional method that we are accustomed to is sending a few hundred dollars extra principal or enroll in the lender's biweekly payment plan in hopes of reducing the total interest and paying off the loan early. I find this to have little impact unless you consistently have the cash to do so.

To understand total interest saved and number of years reduced when making various principal amount payments, an Excel template is set up in *Appendix C.* You can add the amount for extra principal per month and see how the interest and the payoff period change.

I used a range of $50 to $1,000 extra payments per month to model "What if, how much, and how many?" to compare the differences in interest savings and the loan payoff schedule. For example, *what if* I pay an extra $50 per month every month until the loan is paid off. *How much* interest will I save, and by *how many* years will I reduce the loan? I then compare this result to a scenario in which I was not making any extra principal payments. The Excel workbook I created to simulate these scenarios was massive. To spare you the details, only the summary is shown here. The result for each of the corresponding extra principal amount is captured in *Figure 7-4*.

Traditional Method		Paid Off			
EXTRA PRINCIPAL PER MONTH	TOTAL INTEREST PAID	MONTH	YEAR	TOTAL EXTRA PMT	INTEREST SAVED
$0	$238,966	360	30.0		0
$50	$223,379	340	28.3	$17,000	$15,587
$100	$209,817	322	26.8	$32,200	$29,149
$200	$187,316	291	24.3	$58,200	$51,650
$500	$142,385	228	19.0	$114,000	$96,581
$1,000	$102,318	169	14.1	$169,000	$136,648

FIGURE 7—4: Result for each corresponding extra principal amount

If you paid $100 extra principal every month, you'll have saved $29,149 in interest and pay off the loan in a little less than 27 years. Similarly, if you have an extra $1,000 residual income to put toward principal every month, you'll have saved $136,648 in interest and pay off the loan in 14.1 years.

A majority of homeowners can afford to add an extra $100 to $200 per month but not many can add $1,000 month after month. At $200 per month, you'll pay off the loan in 24 years at best. That is still a long time! Let's look at a better option.

Non-Traditional Method—HELOC

The Non-Traditional Method is to leverage HELOC in addition to the regular payment. With this method, you are putting a larger sum toward principal payment, sending it in every few months, which makes it manageable to repay. Since we know that interest is heavily loaded at the beginning of the loan, you are paying off the loan much more quickly by paying a larger sum toward principal early on. It reduces the total interest, thus saving you money. This method works regardless of what your down-payment amount is.

Unless you have inheritance, one sure way to access a larger sum of money is through HELOC. Using Scenario 1, suppose you draw $2,000 or $5,000 from HELOC to pay toward extra principal beginning in the 3rd month after closing on your new home and then continue in the frequency shown in *Figure 7–5*. The pay frequency and the HELOC draw amount are randomly chosen. You can adjust these variables to fit your own situation. The end result is far more favorable than the Traditional Method.

HELOC Method			Paid Off			
PAID IN MONTH	HELOC DRAW AMOUNT	TOTAL INTEREST PAID	MONTH	YEAR	TOTAL EXTRA PMT	INTEREST SAVED
Base	$0	$238,966	360	30.0	NA	NA
3	$2,000	$234,439	356	29.7	$2,000	$4,527
3, 7, 12	$2,000	$225,916	348	29.0	$6,000	$13,050
3, 7, 12, 15, 18, 23, 27, 31, 37, 42, 46, 48, 53, 57 (total 14 months)	$2,000	$189,376	312	26.0	$28,000	$49,590
3, 7, then every 4 months (until loan is paid off)	$3,000	$119,325	194	16.2	$144,000	$119,641
3, 7, then every 4 months (until loan is paid off)	$7,000	$72,720	123	10.3	$210,000	$166,246
3, 7, then every 4 months (until loan is paid off)	$10,000	$56,561	101	8.4	$230,000	$182,405
2, 6, then every 4 months (until loan is paid off)	$5,000	$89,422	150	12.5	$185,000	$149,545

FIGURE 7–5: Using HELOC to reduce mortgage term and save on interest

At first glance, it is not easy to see which method is better. However, if you compare *Figure 7-4* and *Figure 7-5* side-by-side and look closely at the Total Extra Payment and the Paid Off schedule, you will be able to see the differences and determine which method offers more savings in interest and in paying off the loan sooner.

In the Traditional Method, paying an extra $100/month until the loan is paid off in 322 months (26.8 years) means you would have paid extra $32,200 principal. In the HELOC Method, drawing $2,000 in months 3, 7, 12 . . . 57 for 14 months until the loan is paid off in 312 months (26 years) means you would have paid an extra $28,000 in principal. Both of these have relatively close Total Extra Payment Amounts, ($32,000 in Traditional Method vs. $28,000 in HELOC Method) making it close enough for comparison purposes. See *Figure 7–6* below for the differences.

METHODS	TOTAL INTEREST PAID	MONTH	YEAR	TOTAL EXTRA PMT	INTEREST SAVED
Traditional—Extra $100 per month	$209,817	322	26.8	$32,200	$29,149
HELOC—$2,000 every 4 months for months: 3, 7, 12, 15, 18, 23, 27, 31, 37, 42, 46, 48, 53, 57	$189,376	312	26.0	$28,000	$49,590
Difference	($20,441)	(10)	(0.8)	($4,200)	$20,441

FIGURE 7—6: Comparison of Traditional Extra Monthly Principal Method vs. HELOC Method for Scenario 1.

In short, you will pay less in principal, save more in interest, and pay off your mortgage sooner by using the HELOC Method than the Traditional Method. To be exact, you will pay $4,200 less out of pocket to save $20,441 more in interest and project to pay off the loan 10 months sooner than the Traditional Method. Imagine if you continue to repeat this process into the future months. Your interest saved will be significantly more, and you will pay off the debt much sooner. That is the power of HELOC when used in a repetitive cycle! That is how I paid off my mortgage!

I do want to remind you that HELOC is a loan and has interest. How much interest do you pay by borrowing the $28,000 HELOC in order to save $20,441 in the above example? That depends on each person's situation. As explained in Chapter 2, the total HELOC interest is calculated based on average daily balance. Therefore, it depends on your HELOC interest rate, how often and how much you repay, how much your monthly bills are, when you pay those bills, and whether you have unexpected expenses or not. All of these factors affect the total HELOC interest.

To prove that you still come out ahead despite paying at a higher and variable HELOC interest rate, let's look at another analysis and determine whether it is worthwhile to use HELOC to achieve the result in the above example.

HELOC Assumptions:

    HELOC Draw = $2,000 every 4 months

    Draw Frequency = 14 times (month 3, 7, 12, 15, . . . 57)

    HELOC Interest Rate = 7% variable (compares to 4% fixed from the Traditional Method)

    Repay Amount = $500 both interest and principal

    Repay Frequency = every 2 weeks

Based on my own experience, the HELOC interest rate will fluctuate by 0.25% from month to month, or 0.5% every few months, and sometimes no change for months. The HELOC interest rate in this case is purposely chosen at 7%, higher than the 4% fixed used in Scenario 1 for the Traditional Method example.

Using the assumptions above, the cost of borrowing $2,000 HELOC is $9.26. See Excel setup and formula in *Appendix D*. It takes 50 days to repay. Since you have to borrow 14 times, the total HELOC interest is $129.61 ($9.26 x 14). This is the cost of saving $20,441 and shortening the loan by 10 months. In other words, you have an opportunity to save $20,441 by paying $129.61. Not a bad investment.

Again, each of you will have a different situation. Contrary to what most homeowners believe, a variable interest rate is not automatically bad. The above example proves that, even with a higher variable interest rate, such as that which a HELOC has, you are still coming out ahead.

I wanted to test if the HELOC Method benefits people who are not necessarily new homeowners with a new mortgage. Suppose you are years into paying your mortgage. You are more than halfway through the loan, and the principal portion already exceeds the interest portion. If you continue to pay according to the amortization schedule without additional principal payment, what happens, and how long will it take to pay off the loan?

Scenario 2: You own the home for many years.
   House = $350,000
   Down Payment = $70,000 (20%)
   Current Mortgage Balance = $126,607
   Term = 30 years
   Interest rate = 4.0% fixed
   Monthly Payment = $1,336.76

Using the above Scenario 2, let's compare the two methods again and see if the HELOC will outweigh the Traditional Method.

Traditional Method—Extra Monthly Principal
   If you begin to include extra principal each month between $100 and $1,000, as shown in *Figure 7–7*, your balance will be paid off in 5 to 8.8 years. If you make no additional payment, it will take 9.5 years.

Traditional Method			Paid Off			
EXTRA PRINCIPAL PER MONTH	TOTAL INTEREST PAID	MONTH	YEAR	TOTAL EXTRA PMT	INTEREST SAVED
$0	$25,784	114	9.5	0	$0
$100	$23,538	105	8.8	$10,500	$2,245
$200	$21,657	97	8.1	$19,400	$4,127
$500	$17,485	79	6.6	$39,500	$8,299
$1,000	$13,261	60	5.0	$60,000	$12,523

FIGURE 7—7: Total interest saved from extra principal payment.

Non-Traditional Method—HELOC

Suppose you tap into the HELOC and draw $3,000 to $10,000 as in *Figure 7-8*, look at how much quicker you can pay off the loan: 3.6 to 6.6 years.

HELOC Method			Paid Off				
FREQUENCY	HELOC DRAW	TOTAL INTEREST PAID	MONTH	YEAR	# OF PMTS	TOTAL EXTRA PMT	INTEREST SAVED
Start right away, every 6 months	$0	$25,784	114	9.5	0	$0	$0
Start right away, every 6 months	$3,000	$17,113	79	6.6	13	$39,000	$8,671
Start right away, every 6 months	$5,000	$13,910	64	5.3	11	$55,000	$11,873
Start right away, every 6 months	$6,000	$12,708	60	5.0	10	$60,000	$13,076
Start right away, every 6 months	$10,000	$9,383	43	3.6	7	$70,000	$16,400

FIGURE 7—8: Payoff schedule and total interest saved from leveraging HELOC.

If you can afford an extra $500/month toward principal, over 6 months, you would have paid a total of $3,000. This is equivalent to drawing $3,000 every six month from HELOC. You would apply it toward the principal right away, and repeat this cycle every six months. This allows you to repay the HELOC in full before drawing again, while reducing the total interest on the mortgage. It is a much better approach. The comparison is summarized in *Figure 7–9.*

METHODS	TOTAL INTEREST PAID	MONTH	YEAR	TOTAL EXTRA PMT	INTEREST SAVED
Traditional—$500 extra per month	$17,485	79	6.6	$39,500	$8,299
HELOC—$3,000 every 6 months	$17,113	79	6.6	$39,000	$8,671
Differences	($372)	0	0.0	($500)	$372

FIGURE 7—9: Comparison of Traditional Method vs. HELOC Method for Scenario 2

With the Traditional Method of $500 extra principal per month, you will pay off the mortgage in 6.6 years, for a total of $39,500 extra principal. If you use the HELOC Method, your payoff is also in 6.6 years. However, you will pay $500 less in principal and save $372 in interest.

Another analysis is shown in *Figure 7-10.* This example is comparing payment of an extra $1,000 principal per month vs. $6,000 from HELOC every six months. Both methods will take five years to pay off the mortgage. However, you'll pay $553 less in interest with the HELOC Method. Once again, the HELOC is more favorable in both instances.

METHODS	TOTAL INTEREST PAID	MONTH	YEAR	TOTAL EXTRA PMT	INTEREST SAVED
Traditional—$1,000 extra per month	$13,261	60	5.0	$60,000	$12,523
HELOC — $6,000 every 6 months	$12,708	60	5.0	$60,000	$13,076
Differences	($553)	0	0.0	$0	$553

FIGURE 7–10: Comparison of Traditional Extra $1,000 Monthly Principal Method vs. HELOC Method for Scenario 2

While the savings is in this case is not as significant as in the new homeowner's case, the reality is that most homeowners do not have $500–$1,000 extra income month after month to apply toward their mortgages. HELOC offers that solution and you have the flexibility with your repayment.

So, there you have it. Whether you are just beginning your mortgage or are halfway through, and irregardless of what HELOC's interest rate is, it is still a better method for paying off your mortgage sooner.

Below is my personal mortgage record. My husband and I bought the house with a minimum down payment in 2009 and carried a 30-year mortgage of $331,877 at a 5% interest rate. Because we did not put 20% down, we had to pay a monthly PMI. In 2012, we refinanced the balance of $315,000 for a lower interest at 3.25%, also for 30 years. The loan was then sold to different lenders multiple times. Each year, the lender sends out Form-1099, reporting the principal balance, total PMI, and interest paid for tax-return filing. *Figure 7–11* is a summary of ours.

YEAR	BEGINNING BALANCE	TOTAL PMI PAID	TOTAL INTEREST PAID	HELOC INTEREST PAID
2009	$331,877	$6,747	$9,691	NA
2010		$1,766	$17,688	NA
2011		$1,738	$16,058	NA
2012	Refinanced	$1,713	$13,744	NA
2013	$314,860	$1,856	$10,943	NA
2014	$306,730	$1,677	$8,972	NA
2015	$293,274	$1,506	$10,325	NA
2016	$289,177	$1,605	$8,526	NA
2017	$282,580	$1,566	$8,823	NA
2018	$213,030	$1,022	$5,638	NA
2019	$154,970	$0	$1,987	$186
2020	$32,351	$0		$41
TOTAL		$21,198	$112,395	$227

FIGURE 7–11: PMI and Interest Paid on Personal Residential Mortgage

It was astonishing and disappointing to see how much interest we paid—$112,395 in 10 years. Had we not sent in extra principal from time to time and not used the HELOC Method to accelerate the payoff starting in 2019, the interest amount would have continued to grow, and we wouldn't be mortgage-free today. It took 16 months, from January 2019 to February 2020, to pay off the mortgage and then another six weeks to repay the HELOC amount. If I'd known of this technique early on, we wouldn't have paid as much interest as we did. Nonetheless, I am happy that we no longer have to send in another payment.

Now that you have seen the proofs, analyses, and the "what if" scenarios in both the Traditional and the Non-Traditional HELOC methods, where results are substantiated with math, I hope you set up a plan to pay off your mortgage.

I also hope that you will take advantage of the techniques shown in this chapter, this book, and the Excel setup in the Appendices to help you make decisions, improve your financial freedom, and keep some of your hard-earned money instead of giving it to your lender. Becoming mortgage-free is by far one of the biggest milestones in life.

You now have a better understanding of how to leverage HELOC. The next steps are determining what is the right amount to draw, how often to draw, and when to repay it.

Recommended Actions:

1. Re-read this chapter and understand the Traditional Extra Monthly Payment Method vs. the HELOC Method.

2. As an exercise, figure out how much extra principal per month you can put aside to use the HELOC method, or go back and review your residual income.

3. For the Excel gurus, set up your own model using the template and formula in the Appendices referenced in this chapter.

## CHAPTER 8

MANAGING HELOC

Once you are approved for the HELOC, it is available for you to use. You can draw from it immediately by writing HELOC checks or by electronic transfers. The process is relatively easy.

Appropriate Amount and Frequency for Draw

How do you know what is the appropriate amount to draw? That will depend heavily on your residual income. On one hand, it is very tempting to write a check for a large sum to pay toward principal. On the other hand, you do need to consider how long it will take to repay this amount. You still have to make regular monthly payments to your lender in addition to repaying the HELOC. It is important to take this into account.

A quick and effective way to figure out how much to draw is to use a multiplier of your residual income. If you have been tracking your monthly income and expenses as recommended in Chapter 3, then you know what your monthly residual income is. Multiply the residual income by the number of months you anticipate to repay it in full. For example, if you have an average $500 monthly residual income and you want to pay off the HELOC amount in three months, then you should aim to borrow $1,500 ($500 x 3). Repeat the borrow-and-repay cycle.

Depending on your situation and how much you draw, your choices are:

1. Draw a smaller amount, which will allow you to repay the HELOC loan more quickly but have less impact on reducing the mortgage balance, or

2. Draw a larger amount, which will take longer to repay the HELOC loan but will have a greater impact on reducing the mortgage balance. After you experiment with it, you will find a balance that is just right for you.

Pitfalls to Avoid

During my early days with HELOC, I got zealous and drew $10,000 the first time. It became obvious very quickly that I couldn't chip away at the balance—let alone pay it off. My outstanding HELOC balance was accumulating more quickly than I could repay it and it started to incur additional interest. Psychologically, it added stress and pressure. It was very discouraging as it was taking too long to pay it off. After I repaid the amount, I reduced my next draw to $5,000. It became more manageable, and I was able to repay in full within three to five months, sometimes longer. There were times that I had to adjust the amount again due to unexpected repair expenses.

I varied my HELOC draw amount to accommodate my situation. Sometimes I drew $2,000, other times $7,000. There were months in which I sent in only $100 extra principal and did not touch my HELOC until the balance was completely paid off. Once I caught up, I started drawing $5,000 again, paying it off, borrowing, paying it off, and repeating the cycle. I found that drawing $3,000 to $5,000 every three to five months worked for me and, more importantly, I was comfortable with it. I could sleep at night.

You will have to experiment with the draw amount and feel out your comfort level, too. Don't get overly ambitious at the beginning. Start small, and get comfortable with it before increasing the amount. Regardless of the amount that you plan to draw, you can estimate the total HELOC interest in advance by following the calculation and examples in the proceeding chapters and in *Appendix D*.

The most important thing is not to get discouraged if it is not moving as fast as you would like it to. Once you start seeing your mortgage balance decreasing rapidly, you'll know your financial freedom is near.

Repay HELOC

The key to pay off your HELOC balance is to repay as often as you can. This is how you keep the interest to the minimum. Each time you have income coming in, use it to pay off the HELOC. Always repay in full before drawing again.

Emergency Fund

You may ask, "What about saving for emergencies?" At this point, I do not recommend putting money away for emergencies, because that money does not serve you. For example, if you have $5,000 in your saving account for emergencies, you may get a 1% dividend—that is only $50 a year or $4.17 per month. You'd be better off taking that $5,000 and putting it toward the principal. It'll save you more than $50 interest per year, as you saw in the examples from the previous chapter.

In the event that you do need emergency funds, you can tap into the HELOC. The financial gurus out there may not agree with me on this. I emptied my emergency fund to put it toward my principal before using the HELOC method. It was against everything I'd learned. It was very uncomfortable at the beginning, but I took that risk knowing that my job was fairly secure. This was a personal decision. You may be one of those who are very risk-averse and opt to keep the emergency fund. If that's the case, by all means, leave your emergency fund alone. At the end of the day, you have to do what makes you feel comfortable.

Psychological Shift During Payoff

As you begin to use the techniques in this book, you may find yourself adjusting your mindset to achieve your goal. Your overall financial bottom line will not change, but your mental attitude will. We did not have to cut back or make any drastic changes in our lifestyle during the process. However, I, personally, had to accept a psychological shift from being comfortable to being uncomfortable for a short period of time. I was unease with not having emergency funds and relying solely on the HELOC as the backup. My daily checking account balance also dropped from $2,000 to $35 after all bills and HELOCs were paid. This was challenging and uncomfortable at the beginning. I had to adjust my mental attitude to accept the situation as temporary and eagerly await the reward at the end, which was being mortgage-free. With that, my mind became laser focused, and the rest was history.

As you go through your journey, you will encounter some of these shifts. You will have to evaluate and re-evaluate, and then adopt the changes with which you feel comfortable. It is all about *what feels right to you*. It will take time, it will take patience, and it will take focus. If you become focused, you will become mortgage-free.

Recommended Actions:
1. Review your Expense and Incoming Tracking sheet; decide on the HELOC draw amount.
2. Keep the Expense and Income Tracking Sheet updated. Review it periodically to evaluate the residual income and HELOC draw amount.

## CHAPTER 9

IMPLEMENTATION—STEP-BY-STEP TO PAYOFF

You have all of the tools to put the HELOC to use. It is time to implement the process, to make that first lump-sum payment and see how your mortgage balance drops drastically.

If you are able to use HELOC as a checking account, then this option is the easiest. If your lender doesn't permit the use of HELOC as a checking account, you still can achieve the same result, but it requires more coordination and a need to stay on top of managing the cash flowing in and out. Both options are explained below. Regardless of which option you choose, moving all of your monies from a savings to a checking account is the key to reducing the daily interest balance in a HELOC.

Let's start with using a HELOC as a checking account. See *Figure 9–1* and the steps below.

A HELOC as a Checking Account Process:

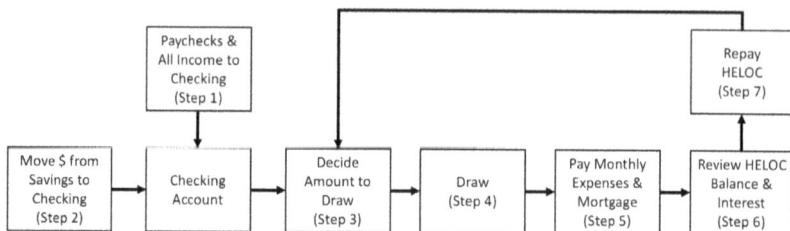

FIGURE 9-1: Using HELOC as a Checking Account

Steps:

1. **Deposit Paychecks and All Income to Checking**—If you have direct deposit, change all of your pay to go to the checking account. If you are receiving paper checks, deposit them into your checking account. This is to make sure all monies are in one location.

2. **Move Monies from Savings to Checking**—If you have separate savings accounts, make sure to move all monies to the checking account. All bills will be paid using the checking account.

3. **Decide Amount to Draw**—Now that all monies are in one place and you know what your monthly residual income is, you can decide on the amount to draw to pay toward principal. I recommend three to five months of residual income. It is more manageable, does not take too long to repay, and makes enough impact on the mortgage payoff.

4. **Draw**—You can either write a HELOC check and mail it to your lender, or you can pay it online from your HELOC account. In either case, you *must* instruct the lender to apply this amount toward *principal only!* Otherwise, they will apply it to the next payment. That is not what you want.

5. **Pay Monthly Expenses and Mortgage**—Although you draw a large sum to pay toward principal in Step 4, you still have to make

your regular monthly mortgage payment as well as pay your normal monthly bills.

6. **Review HELOC Balance and Interest**—It is a good practice to review how much you owe on your HELOC and the total interest you incur on a monthly basis. By reviewing the bank statement, you will also notice interest rate changes, if any.

7. **Repay HELOC**—You will continue to repay the HELOC balance with all of your income. Each time you receive a paycheck, deposit it to your checking account right away. Each dollar that goes in there will reduce the daily balance and the interest.

Once your initial HELOC balance is paid off, repeat Steps three to seven. I strongly recommend that you do not draw another large sum until the HELOC balance is completely paid off. Stick with this process.

Suppose your lender does not offer the option of using HELOC as a checking account. Now what? You still can do it. It has a few extra steps. Here is a rookie mistake that you want to avoid. When I started using HELOC, I linked my credit-card payment to my HELOC account thinking it operates as a checking account. I also changed my direct deposit to go into the HELOC account. Unbeknownst to me, my HELOC cannot be used as a checking account. My direct deposit was rejected, and my credit-card company charged me a late fee for unable to process payment through ACH. Please verify with your lender and don't repeat my mistake. Hopefully, you've already found out the answer early on, having read Chapter 5.

If you cannot use your HELOC as a checking account, the process is still very similar to the above with an additional step. You have to keep two sets of books and exercise some self-discipline. Essentially, you will pay all of your bills and the principal using your HELOC. Then, you can use your checking account to repay your HELOC. This is the extra step. See flow diagram in *Figure 9-2*.

HELOC Cannot Be Used as a Checking Account Process:

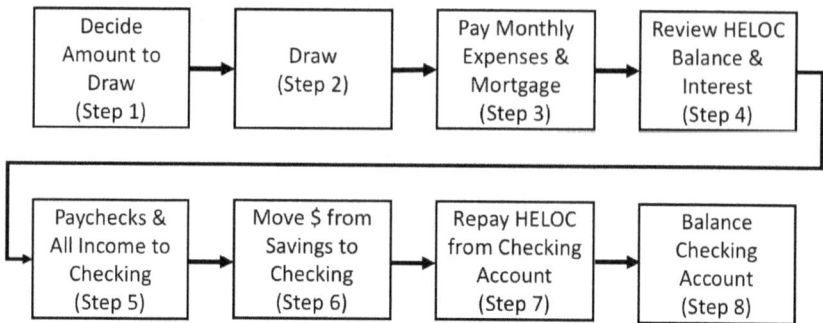

```
┌─────────────┐   ┌─────────────┐   ┌─────────────┐   ┌─────────────┐
│   Decide    │   │             │   │ Pay Monthly │   │Review HELOC │
│  Amount to  │──▶│    Draw     │──▶│ Expenses &  │──▶│  Balance &  │
│    Draw     │   │  (Step 2)   │   │  Mortgage   │   │  Interest   │
│  (Step 1)   │   │             │   │  (Step 3)   │   │  (Step 4)   │
└─────────────┘   └─────────────┘   └─────────────┘   └─────────────┘

┌─────────────┐   ┌─────────────┐   ┌─────────────┐   ┌─────────────┐
│ Paychecks & │   │ Move $ from │   │ Repay HELOC │   │   Balance   │
│ All Income to│──▶│  Savings to │──▶│from Checking│──▶│  Checking   │
│  Checking   │   │  Checking   │   │   Account   │   │   Account   │
│  (Step 5)   │   │  (Step 6)   │   │  (Step 7)   │   │  (Step 8)   │
└─────────────┘   └─────────────┘   └─────────────┘   └─────────────┘
```

FIGURE 9–2: Using HELOC and Checking Separately

Steps:

1. **Decide Amount to Draw**—This is the same as before. Decide on the amount to draw from your HELOC account to pay toward principal. Three to five months of residual income is a good start.

2. **Draw**—You will use the HELOC check to write your large-sum principal. Similar to before, you *must* instruct the lender to apply this amount toward *principal only*! Write on your check "PRINCIPAL ONLY" to avoid any confusion.

3. **Pay Monthly Expenses and Mortgage**—Again, pay all expenses and monthly mortgage with your HELOC checks. If you don't want to write HELOC checks and continue with online payment that links directly to your checking account, you can do so, but it is very important that you balance your checkbook. *You do not want your checking account to go negative.*

4. **Review HELOC Balance and Interest**—Same as before.

5. **Paychecks and All Income to Checking**—same as before, deposit all of your pay to the checking account.

6. **Move Monies from Savings to Checking**—Same as before.

7. **Repay HELOC from Checking Account**—This is where the difference is. Previously you did not have to "pay" HELOC as you would with utilities or other bills by making a transaction. Instead, the repayment was in the form of your monies depositing into the HELOC/Checking account since these two are the same account. In this case where your HELOC and checking are two separate accounts, you have to treat the HELOC balance as another bill and pay it from checking.

8. **Balance Checking Account**—This is an extra step and it is an important one. By balancing your checkbook regularly, you will avoid overdraft and your finance will stay afloat. If you do not keep up with this, it is very easy to lose track and you will incur unnecessary bank fees due to insufficient fund in the checking account. You will become overwhelmed. Self-discipline goes a long way here.

Again, repeat this cycle and only draw after you have repaid the HELOC balance. This process maybe cumbersome at the beginning but you will get the hang of it after a few payments.

CHAPTER 10

THE FINAL MORTGAGE PAYMENT

I T MAY TAKE YOU A FEW MONTHS TO A FEW YEARS to reach the final payoff, depending on the balance of your loan and your HELOC draw, frequency, etc. When you are about to send that final payment, it is undoubtedly the most exciting feeling. Before you mail that check or pay online, make sure to ask your lender about the payoff process. Below is some advice and what to expect:

1. **Payoff Quote**—Call the lender to get a payoff quote. They may charge you a fee, $30 to $50. This fee is for them to calculate the final amount you owe. You may think you already know the final amount. Your final payoff amount will be slightly higher because the lender includes the interest accrued in arrears and the interest good through the final payoff date. They will also add the recording fee. The recording fee is for discharging the lien and transferring the title to you. You will receive a letter with payoff instructions.

2. **Processing Time**—When you call the lender, ask them how long their processing time is to get the payoff quote to you. It should take about three to five business days. Why is the processing time

57

important? Because, if they take too long, you may not have enough time to get the final payment to them by the deadline. Additionally, you need time to coordinate with your bank to either wire the money or obtain a certified check for the payoff amount.

3. **Escrow Fund**—When you were making payments to your lender, they collect escrow to pay your property tax and homeowners' insurance. When you pay off the mortgage, the lender is obligated by law to return any residual escrow funds to you. Ask the lender what their process is and how many days you can expect to see the refund after they received the final payment. Once they return your refund and you cash it, they will officially close your account.

4. **"Good Through" Date**—When you call, your lender will ask what you want your "good through" date to be. The "good through" date is simply the final date that you plan to wire the final payoff to them—that's when the money is physically deposited into their account. They need this information to calculate the total interest up to the date that they anticipate receiving your money. It is not when you mail or postmark the payment. It is the date that the money is shown in their account.

5. **Payoff Method**—Your lender's payoff instructions will be very specific about where and how to send the payment. Make sure you follow them. If your lender requires you to wire the money, make sure you coordinate with your bank, as they need time to set it up. Not all lenders accept certified check, make sure you verify with yours.

A few words when deciding your "good through" date. You need to know your lender's processing time to get you the quote, because it will account the daily interest. For example, let's say you call your lender on the first of the month and ask for a payoff figure. You plan to pay the final amount on the 15th. This means your lender will include the previous month's interest *plus* the interest up to the 15th of the current month. If your lender takes 10 business days to process the payoff quote and it takes another five to seven business days for the payoff package and instructions to get to you, that's a total of 20–22 days. In this case, your plan of paying off the mortgage by the 15th simply won't work. That isn't the worst part. The worst part is that, once the 15th has passed, the lender will continue to charge you interest for each day that they do not receive your payment.

There is an advantage for the "good through" date to be in the first half of the month. You save interest, although the amount is minimal, compared to what you were paying before. The biggest advantage is receiving the escrow refund sooner. My lender's policy is 15 business days to release my escrow fund in the form of a check to me. I requested the "good through" date to be the 14th in order to get my $2,700 escrow refund three weeks from the 14th. I then use this money to pay off the remainder of my HELOC balance. If my "good through" date was at the end of the month, I would need to wait two additional weeks.

It is completely up to you what you want the "good through" date to be. Requesting the end of the month will give you ample time to work with the bank to wire the final payment. It is the safest and easiest way if you don't mind waiting for your escrow refund.

Once you receive the payoff-package instructions, follow it, and wire the fund, or overnight the certified check, depending on your lender's requirement. Congratulations! You've just freed yourself from what was a 30-year mortgage to *zero* payment going forward!

At this time, you can sit back and relax, and just wait for the title and the escrow refund to come through. You will also receive the mortgage discharge. Make sure you keep those documents in a safe place. Imagine the feeling: *You no longer have to pay the monthly mortgage.*

Recommended Action

1. If you are ready to make the final payment, call the lender, and follow the steps above.

CHAPTER 11

AFTER PAYOFF

When you no longer have a mortgage payment, what do you with the HELOC? If you have come this far, you have proven to the lender that you are a responsible consumer. Your choices are endless!

At this point, you can either close the HELOC or keep it open if you a have purpose for it. I closed mine and applied for a higher limit from a different lender that offers more flexibility. My goal is to employ the same techniques and use my HELOC to purchase rental properties.

With the biggest expense removed, your net income should accumulate quickly. Your immediate goals should be to 1) set aside money for property tax and 2) build up your emergency fund.

When you were paying your mortgage, your property tax and homeowner insurance were escrowed into the monthly payment and paid by the lender. Now *you* are responsible for paying the property tax directly to your city and the homeowner insurance to the insurance company. The property tax is a big expense. Make sure you set aside money for it. Depending on when you pay off your mortgage and the time your tax bill is due, you may not have sufficient savings yet. In that case, you may have to draw from the HELOC to pay for the tax until you build up your savings.

For your emergency fund, I recommend eight months' expenses as a cushion. Your new monthly expense no longer includes a mortgage payment, but you do need to add the property tax and homeowner insurance to it. It should not take you long to build up a safety net. The quickest and simplest way to accumulate this money is to shift what once the monthly mortgage payment amount onto a savings account. Continue to track and monitor your personal finances.

Recommended Actions:
1. Set a target amount for your emergency fund.
2. Begin to set aside emergency funds and money for property tax.

CHAPTER 12

WHERE TO GET HELP

It is very rare that you sail through your mortgage payment years without running into any issues with your lender. If this happens, don't get discouraged. This chapter lists the resources that you can turn to for assistance. These agencies exist to protect consumers like you and me. I enlisted their help on multiple occasions; I found them to be very effective and was happy with the result.

I mentioned PMI a few times throughout the book. I am not a fan of it but it does allow one to afford a home with less than 20% down. An FHA loan is such a loan. It requires as little as 3.5% down, which makes this attractive for first-time home buyers or buyers with a small down payment. The trade-off is paying monthly PMI. While this is not the preferred loan for many people, sometimes that is the only option for them. FHA was the only option for me at the time.

FHA loan is different from a conventional loan in that you have to pay a monthly PMI in addition to your PITI. The PMI amount is not fixed; it varies depending on the loan balance. It decreases slightly each month as you pay down the principal. Therefore, you need to pay attention to the PMI amount on your monthly statement. If you refinance and put less than 20% down, the PMI will restart from the beginning. In my case, my PMI started out at $137 per month and decreased to $0 once my loan-to-value reached 78%, or five years, whichever is later. Between the original loan and refinancing, I've paid more than $21,000 in PMI. That is a lot of money. It is the cost of not being able to afford 20% down, but it gave me an opportunity to own a home with only 3.5% down.

To protect yourself and your hard-earned money, you should become familiar with the terms and conditions of your loan. No, you do not need to be a lawyer. If you took out an FHA loan, make a point to know the PMI amount, and understand when you can remove it. Keep a mental note of your equity. If you don't know whether or not it's time to remove it, call your lender to find out. Under FHA loan guidelines, a lender should remove the PMI once you have met the 78% loan-to-value or the five years, whichever is later. It does not always happen, at least not automatically.

Make it your business to mind your own money. As you make your monthly payment, review the principal balance on your statement. If you have surpassed the 22% equity and five years, write to the lender requesting them to remove the PMI. Putting your request in writing is crucial, as it will serve you well if there is a dispute later on. I regret not doing so, and it cost me money and lots of time.

What if you didn't pay attention, and your lender didn't tell you? What if you continue to pay PMI well beyond the 78% loan-to-value ratio and have gone beyond the five years? Can you recoup the money that you overpaid? The answer is "maybe." The key is that you have to ask the lender for it. If you don't ask, you don't get it. Sometimes even when you ask for it, you still won't get it. There are resources out there to help you, but it is up to you to reach out to them. I recommend that you try to resolve any issues directly with your lender before seeking out these resources.

The above scenario happened to me. Almost eighteen months after I had fulfilled my PMI payment obligation, I noticed that I overpaid PMI by $1,408. This discovery was by accident when I was reviewing the account activities. My lesson learned here was that prevention is far better than correction. Trying to get the lender to refund the money was painful, lengthy, and almost impossible. After four months of phone calls, emails, and weekly follow-ups, I was disappointed with the little progress or lack thereof. In desperation, I searched the internet and found Consumer Financial Protection Bureau (CFPB). This is a government agency whose purpose is to help consumers.

Their online process is quick, easy, and very effective. I submitted an online request at https://www.consumerfinance.gov/complaint/, described my problem, and included supportive evidence showing the overpayment claim and the record of phone calls or email communications with my lender. Within five business days, I received a response from CFPB stating that my lender agreed to address the problem. Three weeks later, I received a call from my lender notifying me that they were investigating the matter and expected to give me an update within a few weeks. Shortly afterward, they sent me a letter agreeing to refund the overpayment. That is the effectiveness of CFPB. I did receive my refund.

In addition to CPFB, HUD is also a good place to start if you have an FHA loan. Hopefully, you won't need to go that far. Through my experience, I've learned that the lender collects the monthly PMI from the homeowner, which, in turn, sends or transfers that payment to HUD. Essentially, HUD has the money. When working with HUD, they may at first refuse to work directly with you due to their privacy policy. Their customer is the lender, even though you, the homeowner, are paying the PMI. Sharing information with you would violate the privacy agreement with their customer, the lender. It is understandable. If you need to reach out to HUD, be sure to reference your FHA case number which can be found on your HUD statement as part of the closing package.

Dealing with lenders or government agencies can be frustrating because it takes a long time to resolve a problem. I found it helpful to approach them with respect and courtesy. You can be demanding, but as long as you are respectful, they will cooperate and even go the extra mile to assist you. They have rules and regulations to follow. They have to answer complaint calls all day from people like you and me. Have compassion and be courteous. Treat them the way you want to be treated.

## CHAPTER 13

FINAL REMARKS

In closing, I thank you for giving me the opportunity to share with you what I've learned and what I've developed from my own journey to pay off my mortgage in record time. What I thought would take at least another decade to pay off took only sixteen months. This is truly a surreal accomplishment.

I hope that you will leap forward and reduce years of hard work and save hundreds and thousands of dollars in interest using the methods in this book. Sometimes the best and quickest way to reaching your goal is to learn from other people's success and avoid their mistakes. Knowing that someone has gone through it, took the time to work out the bugs, proved it, and used it to achieve their own dream, you can feel confident that the steps in this book work and that they can help you reach your final destination—and much sooner, too.

As I said at the beginning of the book, we tend to be afraid when we don't understand something. When we are afraid, we hesitate to make decisions. When we don't make decisions, we fail to take action.

When we fail to take action, we miss out on life's opportunities. You now have the information and the techniques in this book to help you make a decision to move forward. Taking the first step will bring you that much closer to your final destination—mortgage freedom.

"Start by doing what's necessary, then do what's possible, and suddenly you are doing the impossible."
—St. Francis of Assisi

ABOUT THE AUTHOR

As a preteen, Lici left her homeland, China, and immigrated to the United States with her family to join her extended family, who live in New York City. At the time, she neither spoke nor read English. She attended school in the Bronx and began learning the alphabet in fifth grade. The language barrier did not deter her from obtaining a higher education. She pursued math and science and received both Bachelor of Science and Master degree in Industrial and Management Engineering from Rensselaer Polytechnic Institute in Troy, New York.

With the desire to explore other parts of the country, she left New York to accept a position in New Hampshire after graduation. Lici has been working in Massachusetts and New Hampshire ever since. She held professions in supply chain, engineering, real estate, operations, and currently in project management. She wants to set an example and inspire others to reach for the impossibles by taking one small step at a time. It all started with a thought.

Appendix A

Excel setup for *Figure 2–2*. Due to space constraints, the amortization schedule shows only the first twelve months.

Purchase Price	$350,000			
Down Payment	$70,000	20%		
Loan	$280,000			
Term (year)	30			
APY	5.00%			
# of Payments/ Year	12			
Monthly Payment	$1,503.10			
Yearly Payment	$18,037.21			
1st Year Total	$18,037.21	$13,906.18	$4,131.02	
30 Years Total	$541,116.20	$261,116.20	$280,000.00	
MONTH	**PAYMENT**	**INTEREST**	**PRINCIPAL**	**ENDING BALANCE**
1	$1,503.10	$1,166.67	$336.43	$279,663.57
2	$1,503.10	$1,165.26	$337.84	$279,325.73
3	$1,503.10	$1,163.86	$339.24	$278,986.49
4	$1,503.10	$1,162.44	$340.66	$278,645.83
5	$1,503.10	$1,161.02	$342.08	$278,303.75
6	$1,503.10	$1,159.60	$343.50	$277,960.25
7	$1,503.10	$1,158.17	$344.93	$277,615.32
8	$1,503.10	$1,156.73	$346.37	$277,268.95
9	$1,503.10	$1,155.29	$347.81	$276,921.14
10	$1,503.10	$1,153.84	$349.26	$276,571.87
11	$1,503.10	$1,152.38	$350.72	$276,221.16
12	$1,503.10	$1,150.92	$352.18	$275,868.98

Formula for *Figure 2–2*

Purchase Price	350000	
Down Payment	=C3*B2	0.2
Loan	=B2-B3	
Term (year)	30	
APY	0.05	
# of Payments/Year	12	
Monthly Payment	=PMT(B6/B7,B5*B7,-B4)	
Yearly Payment	=B8*12	

Month	Payment	Interest	Principal	Ending Balance
1st Year Total	=SUM(B14:B25)	=SUM(C14:C25)	=SUM(D14:D25)	
30 Years Total	=SUM(B14:B373)	=SUM(C14:C373)	=SUM(D14:D373)	
1	=$B$8	=$B$6/$B$7*$B$4	=B14-C14	=B4-D14
2	=$B$8	=$B$6/$B$7*E14	=B15-C15	=E14-D15
3	=$B$8	=$B$6/$B$7*E15	=B16-C16	=E15-D16
4	=$B$8	=$B$6/$B$7*E16	=B17-C17	=E16-D17
5	=$B$8	=$B$6/$B$7*E17	=B18-C18	=E17-D18
6	=$B$8	=$B$6/$B$7*E18	=B19-C19	=E18-D19
7	=$B$8	=$B$6/$B$7*E19	=B20-C20	=E19-D20
8	=$B$8	=$B$6/$B$7*E20	=B21-C21	=E20-D21
9	=$B$8	=$B$6/$B$7*E21	=B22-C22	=E21-D22
10	=$B$8	=$B$6/$B$7*E22	=B23-C23	=E22-D23
11	=$B$8	=$B$6/$B$7*E23	=B24-C24	=E23-D24
12	=$B$8	=$B$6/$B$7*E24	=B25-C25	=E24-D25

Appendix B

Excel setup for *Figure 6–1*. Due to space constraints, the amortization schedule shows only the first twelve months.

House Purchase Price	$350,000			
Down Payment	$17,500	5%		
Mortgage	$332,500			
Term (year)	30			
APY (interest rate)	4.00%			
# of Payments/ Year	12			
Monthly Payment	$1,587.41			
Extra Principal/ Month	$0			
Count		360		
1st Year Total	$19,048.87	$13,193.42	$5,855.45	
30 Years Total	$571,466.11	$238,966.11	$332,500.00	
MONTH	**PAYMENT**	**INTEREST**	**PRINCIPAL**	**ENDING BALANCE**
1	$1,587.41	$1,108.33	$479.07	$332,020.93
2	$1,587.41	$1,106.74	$480.67	$331,540.26
3	$1,587.41	$1,105.13	$482.27	$331,057.99
4	$1,587.41	$1,103.53	$483.88	$330,574.11
5	$1,587.41	$1,101.91	$485.49	$330,088.61
6	$1,587.41	$1,100.30	$487.11	$329,601.50
7	$1,587.41	$1,098.67	$488.73	$329,112.77
8	$1,587.41	$1,097.04	$490.36	$328,622.41
9	$1,587.41	$1,095.41	$492.00	$328,130.41
10	$1,587.41	$1,093.77	$493.64	$327,636.77
11	$1,587.41	$1,092.12	$495.28	$327,141.49
12	$1,587.41	$1,090.47	$496.93	$326,644.55

Formula for *Figure 6–1*

House Purchase Price	350000	
Down Payment	=B2*C3	0.05
Mortgage	=B2-B3	
Term (year)	30	
APY (interest rate)	0.04	
# of Payments/Year	12	
Monthly Payment	=PMT(B6/B7,B5*B7,-B4)	

Extra Principal/Month   0

	Payment	Interest	Principal	Ending Balance	Lump-Sum
Count		=COUNT(C17:C376)			
1st Year Total	=SUM(B17:B28)	=SUM(C17:C28)	=SUM(D17:D28)		
30 Years Total	=SUM(B17:B376)	=SUM(C17:C376)	=SUM(D17:D376)		=SUM(F17:F376)
Month	Payment	Interest	Principal	Ending Balance	Lump-Sum
1	=$B$8	=$B$6/$B$7*$B$54	=B17-C17+$B$10+F17	=B4-D17	
2	=$B$8	=$B$6/$B$7*E17	=B18-C18+$B$10+F18	=E17-D18	
3	=$B$8	=$B$6/$B$7*E18	=B19-C19+$B$10+F19	=E18-D19	
4	=$B$8	=$B$6/$B$7*E19	=B20-C20+$B$10+F20	=E19-D20	
5	=$B$8	=$B$6/$B$7*E20	=B21-C21+$B$10+F21	=E20-D21	
6	=$B$8	=$B$6/$B$7*E21	=B22-C22+$B$10+F22	=E21-D22	
7	=$B$8	=$B$6/$B$7*E22	=B23-C23+$B$10+F23	=E22-D23	
8	=$B$8	=$B$6/$B$7*E23	=B24-C24+$B$10+F24	=E23-D24	
9	=$B$8	=$B$6/$B$7*E24	=B25-C25+$B$10+F25	=E24-D25	
10	=$B$8	=$B$6/$B$7*E25	=B26-C26+$B$10+F26	=E25-D26	
11	=$B$8	=$B$6/$B$7*E26	=B27-C27+$B$10+F27	=E26-D27	
12	=$B$8	=$B$6/$B$7*E27	=B28-C28+$B$10+F28	=E27-D28	

Excel setup for *Figure 6–2*. Due to space constraints, the amortization schedule shows only the first twelve months.

House Purchase Price	$350,000				
Down Payment	$17,500	5%			
Mortgage	$332,500				
Term (year)	30				
APY (interest rate)	4.00%				
# of Payments/ Year	12				
Monthly Payment	$1,587.41				
Extra Principal/ Month	$0				
Count		356			1
1st Year Total	$19,048.87	$13,132.62	$7,916.25		
29.7 Years Total	$564,939.14	$234,439.14	$332,500.00		$2,000.00
MONTH	PAYMENT	INTEREST	PRINCIPAL	ENDING BALANCE	LUMP-SUM
1	$1,587.41	$1,108.33	$479.07	$332,020.93	
2	$1,587.41	$1,106.74	$480.67	$331,540.26	
3	$1,587.41	$1,105.13	$2,482.27	$329,057.99	$2,000.00
4	$1,587.41	$1,096.86	$490.55	$328,567.44	
5	$1,587.41	$1,095.22	$492.18	$328,075.26	
6	$1,587.41	$1,093.58	$493.82	$327,581.44	
7	$1,587.41	$1,091.94	$495.47	$327,085.97	
8	$1,587.41	$1,090.29	$497.12	$326,588.85	
9	$1,587.41	$1,088.63	$498.78	$326,090.07	
10	$1,587.41	$1,086.97	$500.44	$325,589.64	
11	$1,587.41	$1,085.30	$502.11	$325,087.53	
12	$1,587.41	$1,083.63	$503.78	$324,583.75	

Formula for *Figure 6–2*

House Purchase Price	350000	
Down Payment	=B2*C3	0.05
Mortgage	=B2-B3	
Term (year)	30	
APY (interest rate)	0.04	
# of Payments/Year	12	
Monthly Payment	=PMT(B6/B7,B5*B7, B4)	

Extra Principal/Month   0

	Count		=COUNT(C17:C372)			=COUNT(F17:F376)
	1st Year Total	=SUM(B17:B28)	=SUM(C17:C28)	=SUM(D17:D28)		
	29.7 Years Total	=SUM(B17:B372)	=SUM(C17:C372)	=SUM(D17:D372)		=SUM(F17:F376)
	Month	Payment	Interest	Principal	Ending Balance	Lump-Sum
1		=$B$8	=$B$6/$B$7*$B$4	=B17-C17+$B$10+F17	=B4-D17	
2		=$B$8	=$B$6/$B$7*E17	=B18-C18+$B$10+F18	=E17-D18	
3		=$B$8	=$B$6/$B$7*E18	=B19-C19+$B$10+F19	=E18-D19	2000
4		=$B$8	=$B$6/$B$7*E19	=B20-C20+$B$10+F20	=E19-D20	
5		=$B$8	=$B$6/$B$7*E20	=B21-C21+$B$10+F21	=E20-D21	
6		=$B$8	=$B$6/$B$7*E21	=B22-C22+$B$10+F22	=E21-D22	
7		=$B$8	=$B$6/$B$7*E22	=B23-C23+$B$10+F23	=E22-D23	
8		=$B$8	=$B$6/$B$7*E23	=B24-C24+$B$10+F24	=E23-D24	
9		=$B$8	=$B$6/$B$7*E24	=B25-C25+$B$10+F25	=E24-D25	
10		=$B$8	=$B$6/$B$7*E25	=B26-C26+$B$10+F26	=E25-D26	
11		=$B$8	=$B$6/$B$7*E26	=B27-C27+$B$10+F27	=E26-D27	
12		=$B$8	=$B$6/$B$7*E27	=B28-C28+$B$10+F28	=E27-D28	

Appendix C

Excel setup for paying Extra Principal per Month scenario in *Figure 7–4*. Due to space constraints, the amortization schedule shows only the first twelve months.

Paying Extra $100/Month Principal				
House Purchase Price	$350,000			
Down Payment	$17,500			
Mortgage	$332,500			
Term (year)	30	5%		
APY (interest rate)	4.00%			
# of Payments/ Year	12			
Monthly Payment	$1,587.41			
Extra Principal/ Month	$100			
# of Extra Principal Payment	321			
Count		322		
Total	$510,217	$209,817	$332,500	
MONTH	PAYMENT	INTEREST	PRINCIPAL	ENDING BALANCE
1	$1,587.41	$1,108.33	$579.07	$331,920.93
2	$1,587.41	$1,106.40	$581.00	$331,339.92
3	$1,587.41	$1,104.47	$582.94	$330,756.99
4	$1,587.41	$1,102.52	$584.88	$330,172.10
5	$1,587.41	$1,100.57	$586.83	$329,585.27
6	$1,587.41	$1,098.62	$588.79	$328,996.48
7	$1,587.41	$1,096.65	$590.75	$328,405.73
8	$1,587.41	$1,094.69	$592.72	$327,813.01
9	$1,587.41	$1,092.71	$594.70	$327,218.32
10	$1,587.41	$1,090.73	$596.68	$326,621.64
11	$1,587.41	$1,088.74	$598.67	$326,022.97
12	$1,587.41	$1,086.74	$600.66	$325,422.31

Appendix C

Formula for paying Extra Principal per Month scenario in *Figure 7–4*.

Paying Extra $100/Month Principal

House Purchase Price	350000				
Down Payment	=B2*C5				
Mortgage	=B2-B3				
Term (year)	30	0.05			
APY (interest rate)	0.04				
# of Payments/Year	12				
Monthly Payment	=PMT(B6/B7,B5*B7,-B4)				
Extra Principal/Month	100				
# of Extra Principal Payments	=C15-1				

		Count		=COUNT(C18:C339)		
		Total	=SUM(B18:B339)	=SUM(C18:C339)	=SUM(D18:D339)	
		Month	**Payment**	**Interest**	**Principal**	**Ending Balance**
	1		=$B$8	=$B$6/$B$7*$B$4	=B18-C18+$B$10	=B4-D18
	2		=$B$8	=$B$6/$B$7*E18	=B19-C19+$B$10	=E18-D19
	3		=$B$8	=$B$6/$B$7*E19	=B20-C20+$B$10	=E19-D20
	4		=$B$8	=$B$6/$B$7*E20	=B21-C21+$B$10	=E20-D21
	5		=$B$8	=$B$6/$B$7*E21	=B22-C22+$B$10	=E21-D22
	6		=$B$8	=$B$6/$B$7*E22	=B23-C23+$B$10	=E22-D23
	7		=$B$8	=$B$6/$B$7*E23	=B24-C24+$B$10	=E23-D24
	8		=$B$8	=$B$6/$B$7*E24	=B25-C25+$B$10	=E24-D25
	9		=$B$8	=$B$6/$B$7*E25	=B26-C26+$B$10	=E25-D26
	10		=$B$8	=$B$6/$B$7*E26	=B27-C27+$B$10	=E26-D27
	11		=$B$8	=$B$6/$B$7*E27	=B28-C28+$B$10	=E27-D28
	12		=$B$8	=$B$6/$B$7*E28	=B29-C29+$B$10	=E28-D29

Excel setup for scenario in *Figure 7–5*. Due to space constraints, the amortization schedule shows only the first twelve months.

Draw HELOC in month: 3, 7, 12, 15, 18, 23, 27, 31, 37, 42, 46, 48, 53, 57					
House Purchase Price	$350,000				
Down Payment	$17,500	5%			
Mortgage	$332,500				
Term (year)	30				
APY (interest rate)	4.00%				
# of Payments/ Year	12				
Monthly Payment	$1,587.41				
Extra Principal/ Month					
# of Extra Principal Payments	311				
Count		312			14
Total	$493,876	$189,376	$332,500		$28,000
MONTH	**PAYMENT**	**INTEREST**	**PRINCIPAL**	**ENDING BALANCE**	**LUMP-SUM**
1	$1,587.41	$1,108.33	$479.07	$332,020.93	
2	$1,587.41	$1,106.74	$480.67	$331,540.26	
3	$1,587.41	$1,105.13	$2,482.27	$329,057.99	$2,000.00
4	$1,587.41	$1,096.86	$490.55	$328,567.44	
5	$1,587.41	$1,095.22	$492.18	$328,075.26	
6	$1,587.41	$1,093.58	$493.82	$327,581.44	
7	$1,587.41	$1,091.94	$2,495.47	$325,085.97	$2,000.00
8	$1,587.41	$1,083.62	$503.79	$324,582.18	
9	$1,587.41	$1,081.94	$505.47	$324,076.72	
10	$1,587.41	$1,080.26	$507.15	$323,569.57	
11	$1,587.41	$1,078.57	$508.84	$323,060.73	
12	$1,587.41	$1,076.87	$2,510.54	$320,550.19	$2,000.00

Formula for scenario in *Figure 7–5*

Draw HELOC in month: 3, 7, 12, 15, 18, 23, 27, 31, 37, 42, 46, 48, 53, 57

House Purchase Price	350000	
Down Payment	=B2*C3	0.05
Mortgage	=B2-B3	
Term (year)	30	
APY (interest rate)	0.04	
# of Payments/Year	12	
Monthly Payment	=PMT(B6/B7,B5*B7,-B4)	
Extra Principal/Month		
# of Extra Principal Payments	=C14-1	

	Count		=COUNT(C17:C328)			=COUNT(F17:F376)
	Total	=SUM(B17:B328)	=SUM(C17:C328)	=SUM(D17:D328)		=SUM(F17:F376)
	Month	Payment	Interest	Principal	Ending Balance	Lump-Sum
1		=$B$8	=$B$6/$B$7*$B$4	=B17-C17+$B$10+F17	=B4-D17	
2		=$B$8	=$B$6/$B$7*E17	=B18-C18+$B$10+F18	=E17-D18	
3		=$B$8	=$B$6/$B$7*E18	=B19-C19+$B$10+F19	=E18-D19	2000
4		=$B$8	=$B$6/$B$7*E19	=B20-C20+$B$10+F20	=E19-D20	
5		=$B$8	=$B$6/$B$7*E20	=B21-C21+$B$10+F21	=E20-D21	
6		=$B$8	=$B$6/$B$7*E21	=B22-C22+$B$10+F22	=E21-D22	
7		=$B$8	=$B$6/$B$7*E22	=B23-C23+$B$10+F23	=E22-D23	2000
8		=$B$8	=$B$6/$B$7*E23	=B24-C24+$B$10+F24	=E23-D24	
9		=$B$8	=$B$6/$B$7*E24	=B25-C25+$B$10+F25	=E24-D25	
10		=$B$8	=$B$6/$B$7*E25	=B26-C26+$B$10+F26	=E25-D26	
11		=$B$8	=$B$6/$B$7*E26	=B27-C27+$B$10+F27	=E26-D27	
12		=$B$8	=$B$6/$B$7*E27	=B28-C28+$B$10+F28	=E27-D28	2000

Appendix D

Excel setup to repay a $2,000 HELOC at the following assumptions.

Assumptions:

HELOC Draw = $2,000

Draw Frequency = 14 times

HELOC Interest Rate = 7% variable

Repay Amount = $500 both interest and principal

Repay Frequency = every 10 calendar days

Due to space constraints, only partial calculation is shown here. Excel user can repeat payment until entire $2,000 is paid off.

Assumption:					
HELOC Amount	$2,000		Total Borrow Amount	$28,000	
Interest Rate	7.00%		Borrow Frequency	14	
Repay every 10 days (P&I)	500		Total HELOC Interest	$129.61	
Paid off in # of days	50				
Total		$2,000.02		$9.26	$9.26
DATE	**DRAW**	**PAYMENT**	**BALANCE**	**DAILY INTEREST**	**TOTAL INTEREST**
3/1			$2,000.00	$0.38	
3/2			$2,000.00	$0.38	
3/3			$2,000.00	$0.38	
3/4			$2,000.00	$0.38	
3/5			$2,000.00	$0.38	
3/6			$2,000.00	$0.38	
3/7			$2,000.00	$0.38	
3/8			$2,000.00	$0.38	
3/9			$2,000.00	$0.38	
3/10		$496.55	$1,503.45	$0.29	$3.45
3/11			$1,503.45	$0.29	
3/12			$1,503.45	$0.29	
3/13			$1,503.45	$0.29	
3/14			$1,503.45	$0.29	
3/15			$1,503.45	$0.29	
3/16			$1,503.45	$0.29	
3/17			$1,503.45	$0.29	
3/18			$1,503.45	$0.29	
3/19			$1,503.45	$0.29	
3/19		$497.12	$1,006.34	$0.19	$2.88

The Mortgage Freedom Playbook

Formula

Assumption:

HELOC Amount	2000		Total Borrow Amount	=28000
Interest Rate	0.07		Borrow Frequency	=E3/B3
Repay every 10 days (P&I)	500		Total HELOC Interest	=E4*E8
Paid off in # of days	=COUNT(A10:A59)			

Total			=SUM(C10:C59)		=SUM(E10:E59)	=SUM(F10:F59)
Date	Draw	Payment		Balance	Daily interest	Total Interest
43891				=B3	=$B$4/365*D10	
43892				=D10+B11-C11	=$B$4/365*D11	
43893				=D11+B12-C12	=$B$4/365*D12	
43894				=D12+B13-C13	=$B$4/365*D13	
43895				=D13+B14-C14	=$B$4/365*D14	
43896				=D14+B15-C15	=$B$4/365*D15	
43897				=D15+B16-C16	=$B$4/365*D16	
43898				=D16+B17-C17	=$B$4/365*D17	
43899				=D17+B18-C18	=$B$4/365*D18	
43900		=$B$5-F19		=D18+B19-C19	=$B$4/365*D19	=SUM(E10:E18)
43901				=D19+B20-C20	=$B$4/365*D20	
43902				=D20+B21-C21	=$B$4/365*D21	
43903				=D21+B22-C22	=$B$4/365*D22	
43904				=D22+B23-C23	=$B$4/365*D23	
43905				=D23+B24-C24	=$B$4/365*D24	
43906				=D24+B25-C25	=$B$4/365*D25	
43907				=D25+B26-C26	=$B$4/365*D26	
43908				=D26+B27-C27	=$B$4/365*D27	
43909				=D27+B28-C28	=$B$4/365*D28	
43910		=$B$5-F29		=D28+B29-C29	=$B$4/365*D29	=SUM(E19:E28)